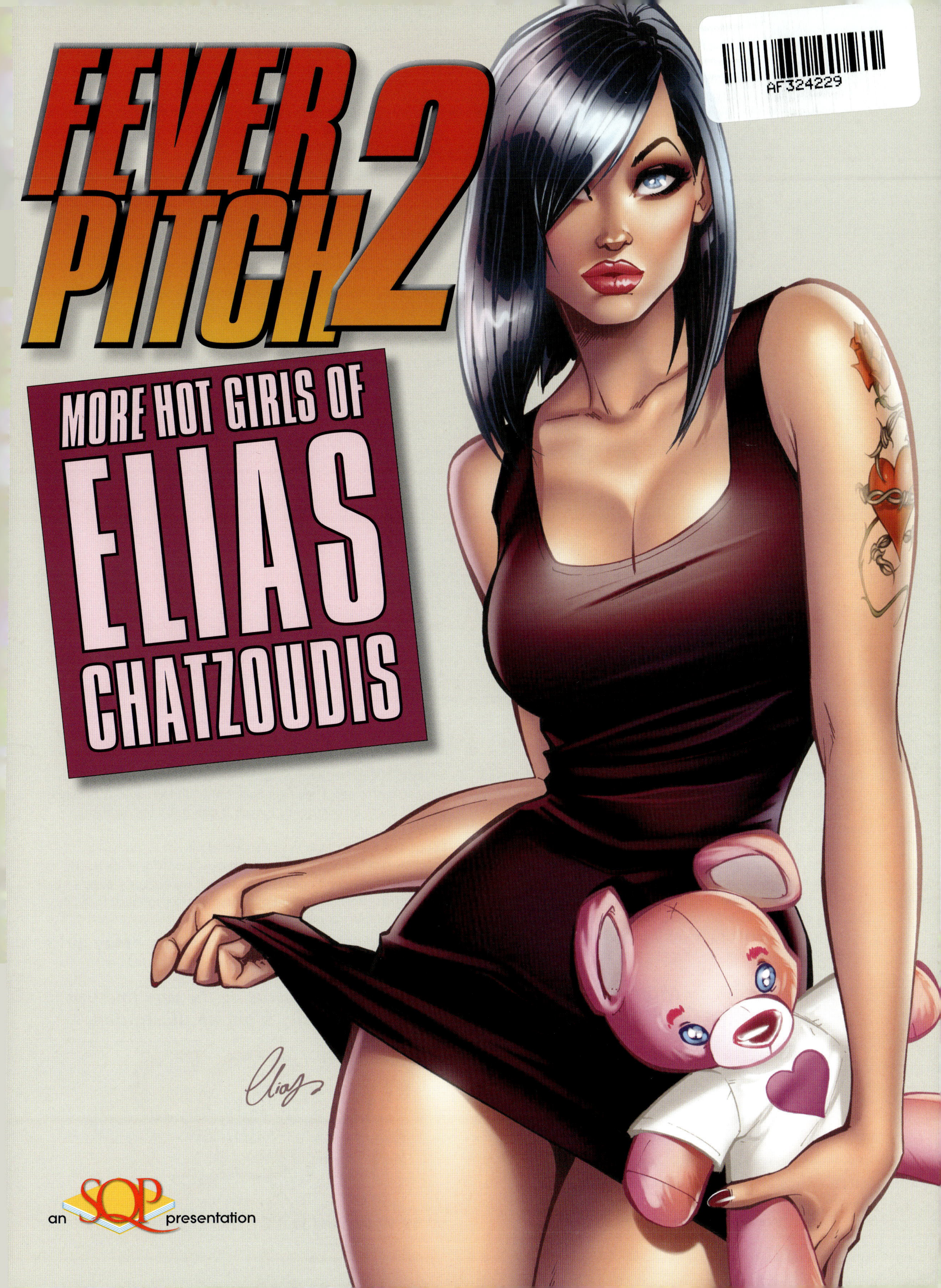

FEVER PITCH 2
MORE HOT GIRLS OF
ELIAS
CHATZOUDIS
AF324229
an SQP presentation

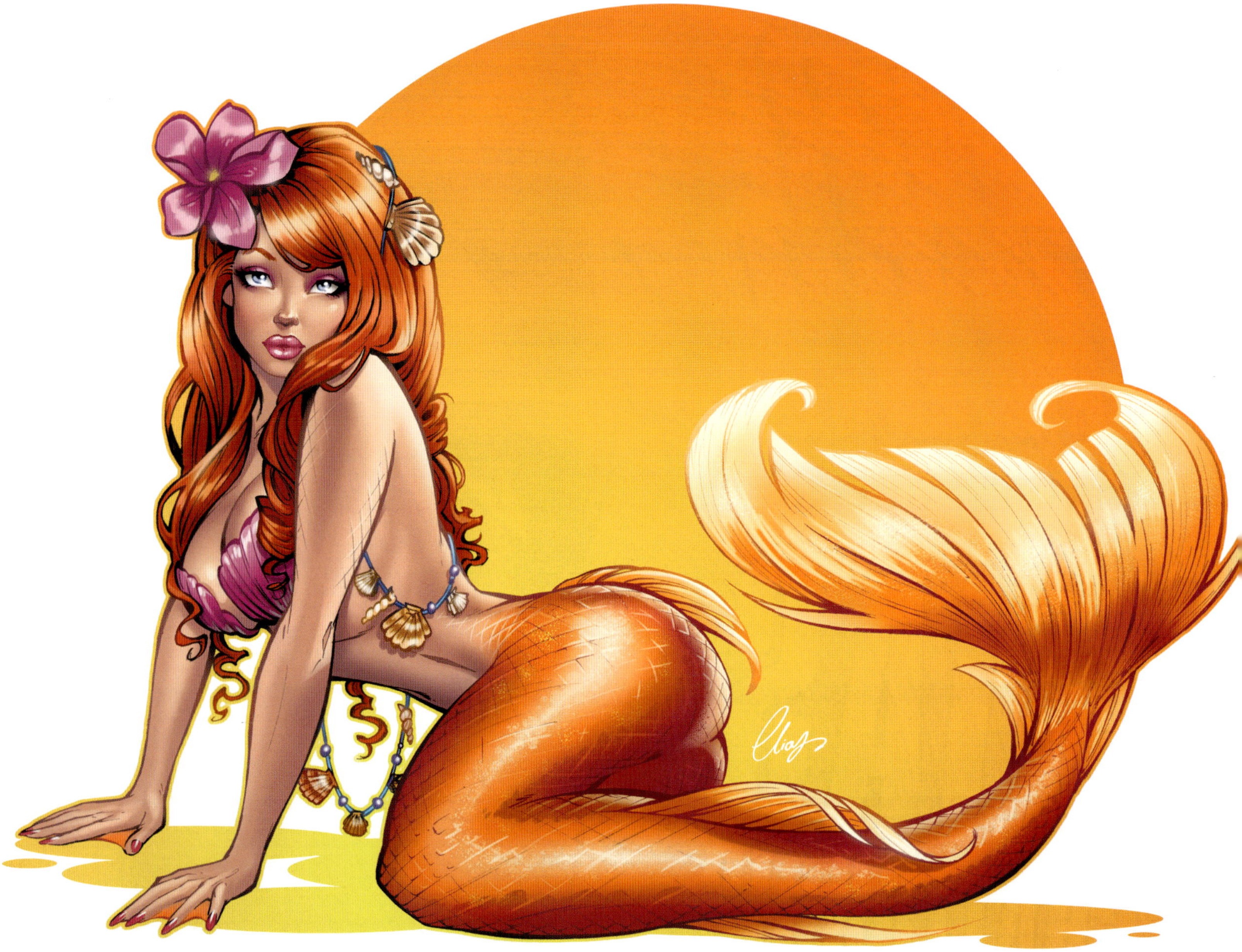

Fever Pitch 2 - *Hotter than Ever!*

Nothing succeeds like success, and my first collection of pin-ups in "Fever Pitch 1" met with the kind of reaction an artist is always happy to get from fans - absolute delight mixed with an impossible impatience for the NEXT book! That's fine - luckily I work quickly and enjoy what I do.

It's been just over a year since that first book, and in that time, I've been able to attend several conventions, including ones in London and New York. It's one thing to sit alone in my studio working deep into the night - it's quite another sensation to meet my fans in person, and receive such terrific attention and feedback! I get the "Rock Star" treatment at these shows, which is great for my ego. Then I get back home and am quickly brought back to Earth by my friends (which is also good for my ego!)

I hope you enjoy this latest selection of new sexy sirens - I certainly had fun bringing them into existence! For daily, hourly, or second-by-second updates, please visit my personal page *www.elias-design.gr*. And of course, thanks so much for your constant support and interest!

Elias Chatzoudis - May 2013

Fever Pitch 2 - More Hot Girls of Elias Chatzoudis

Since 1973, showcasing the very finest in fantasy, erotic, & pin-up illustration.

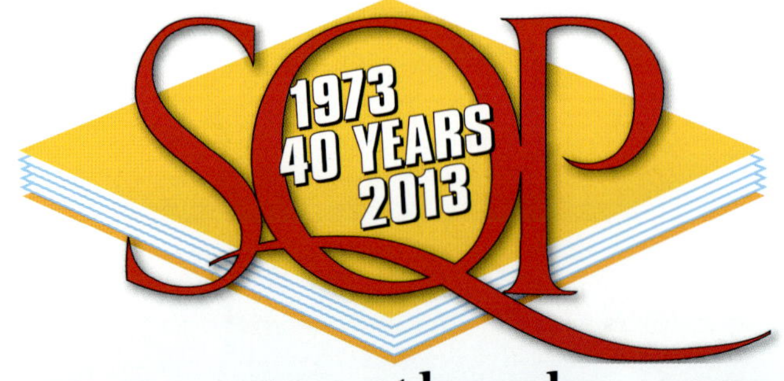

www.sqpartbooks.com

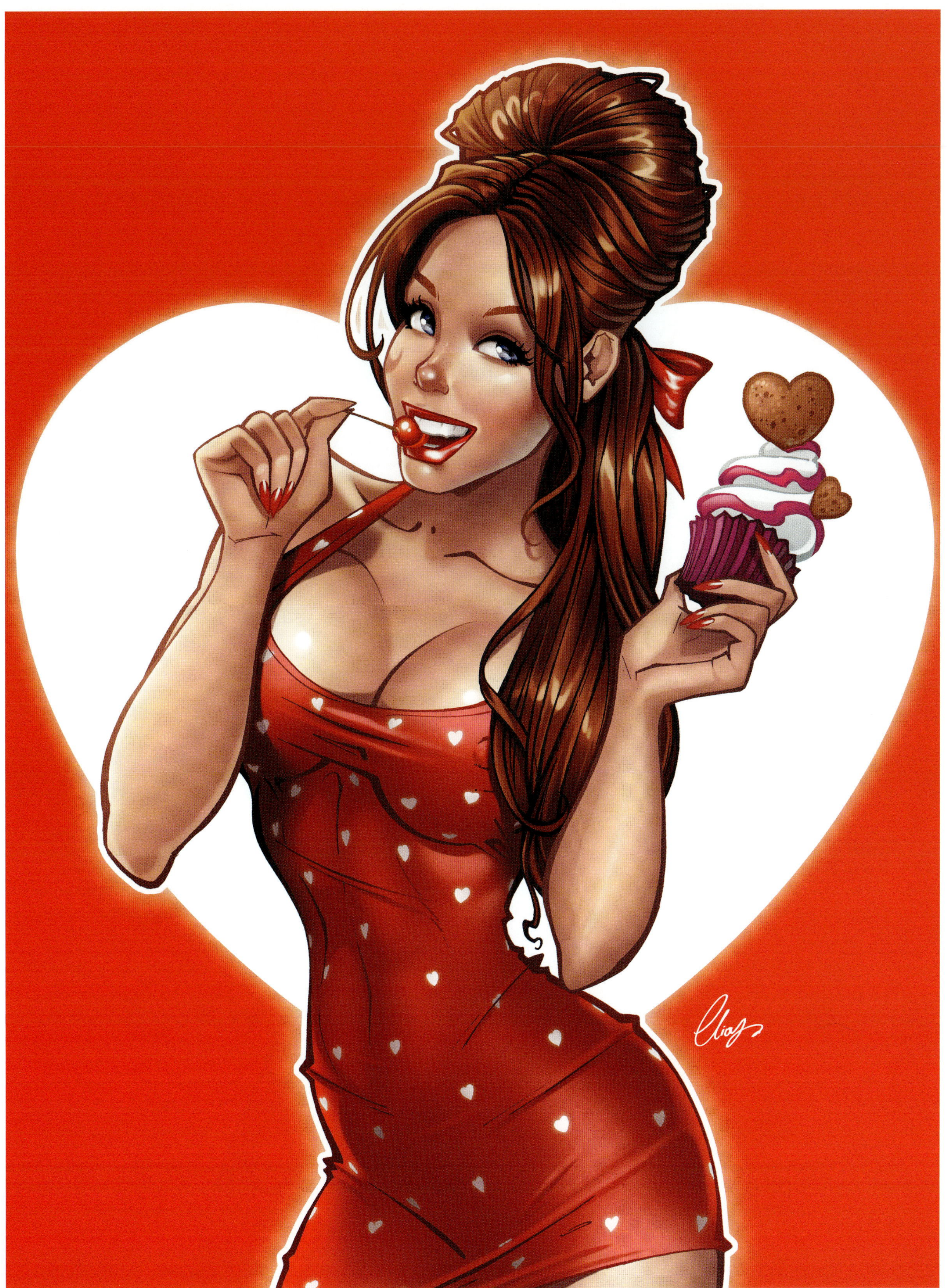

Love Cup Cake

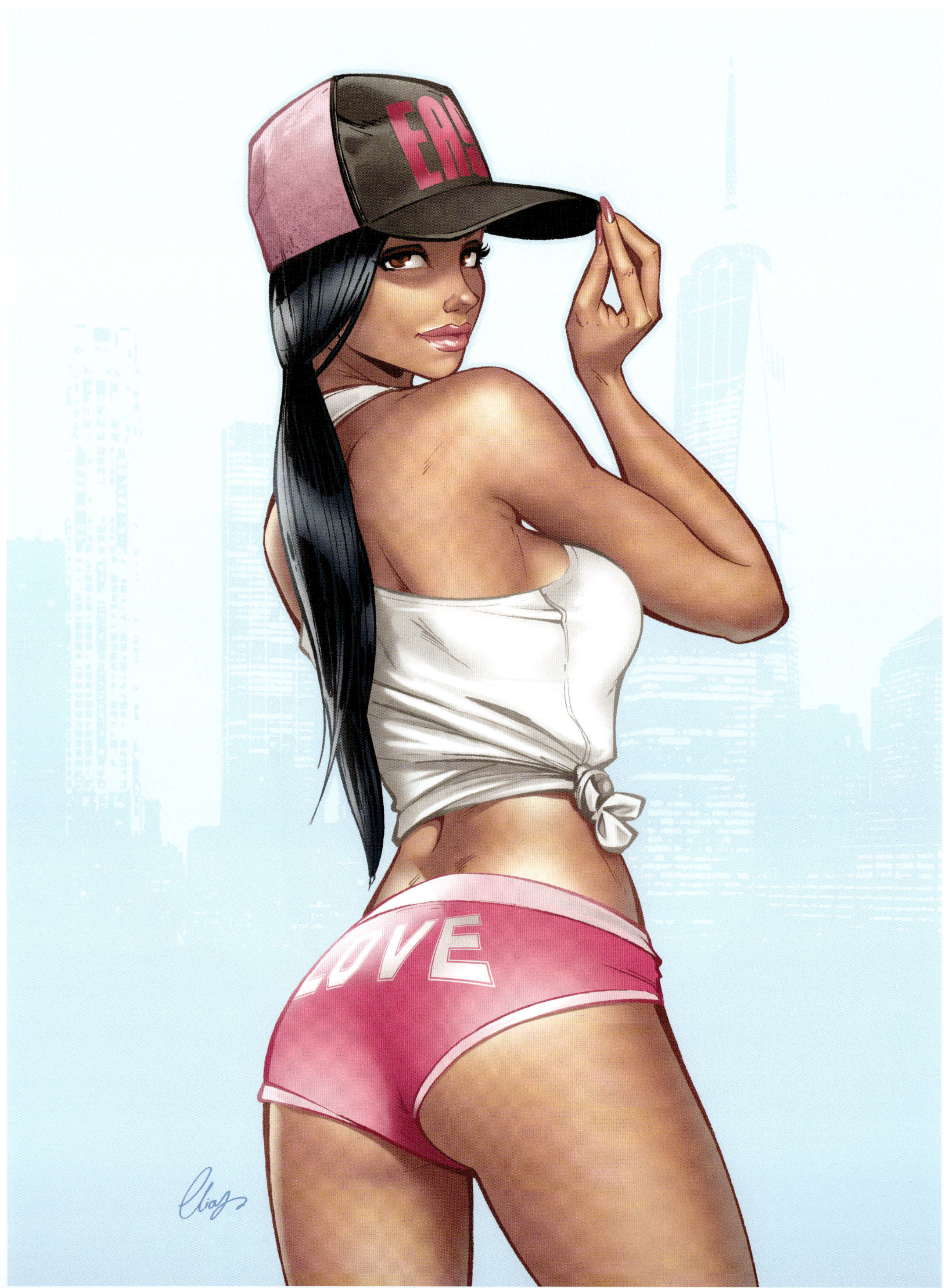

Love

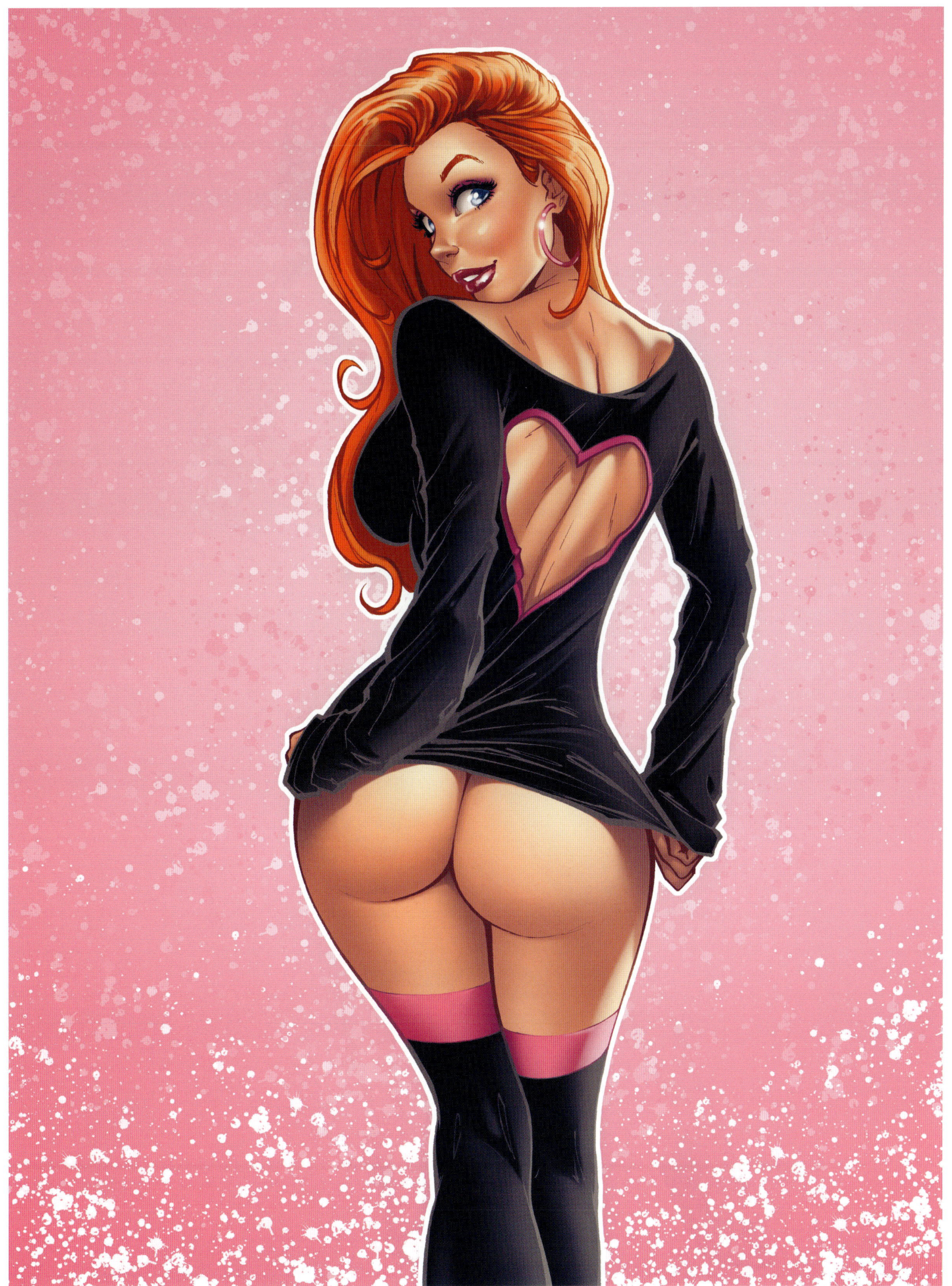

Isabella

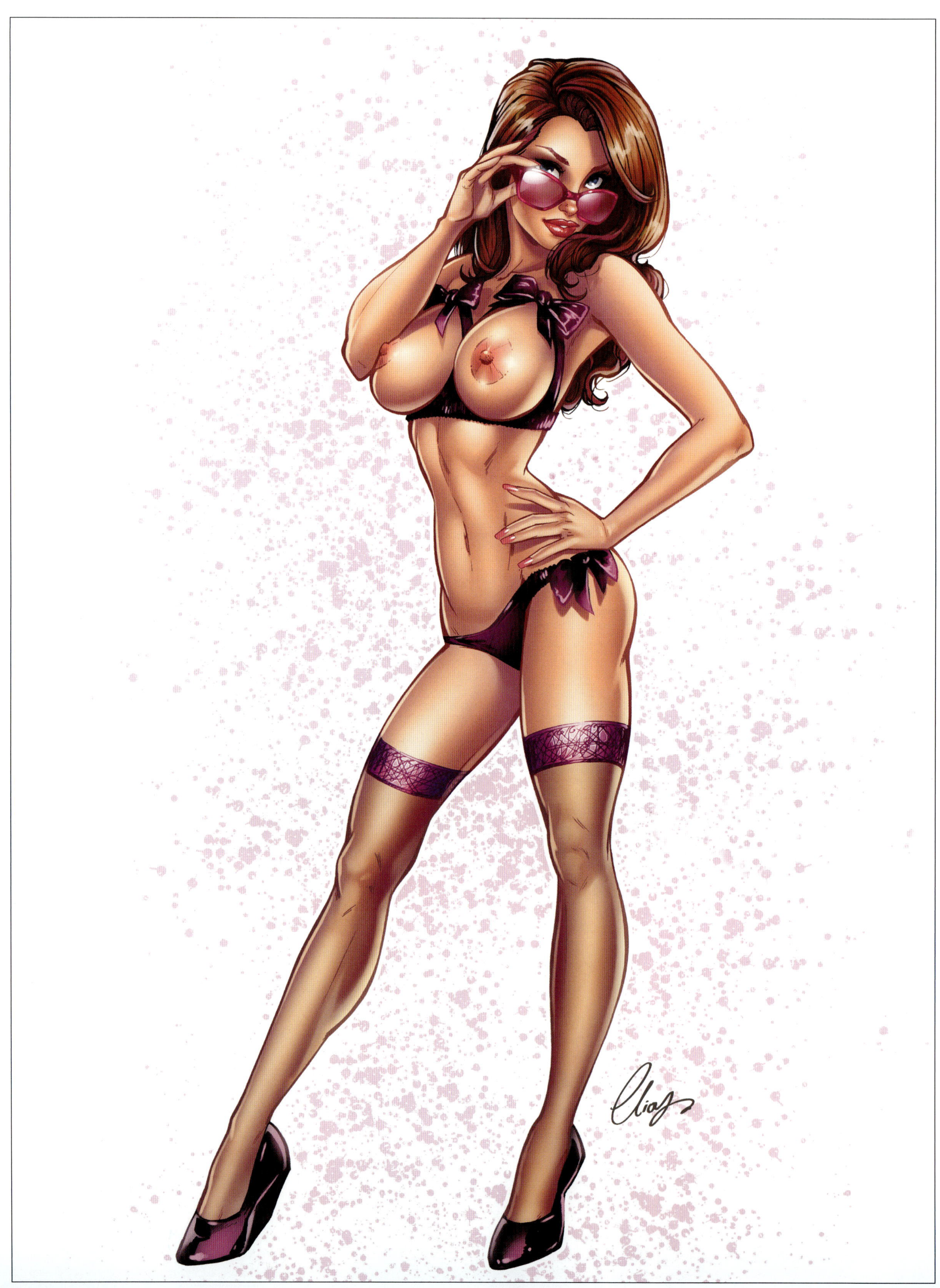

Are You Talking To Me?

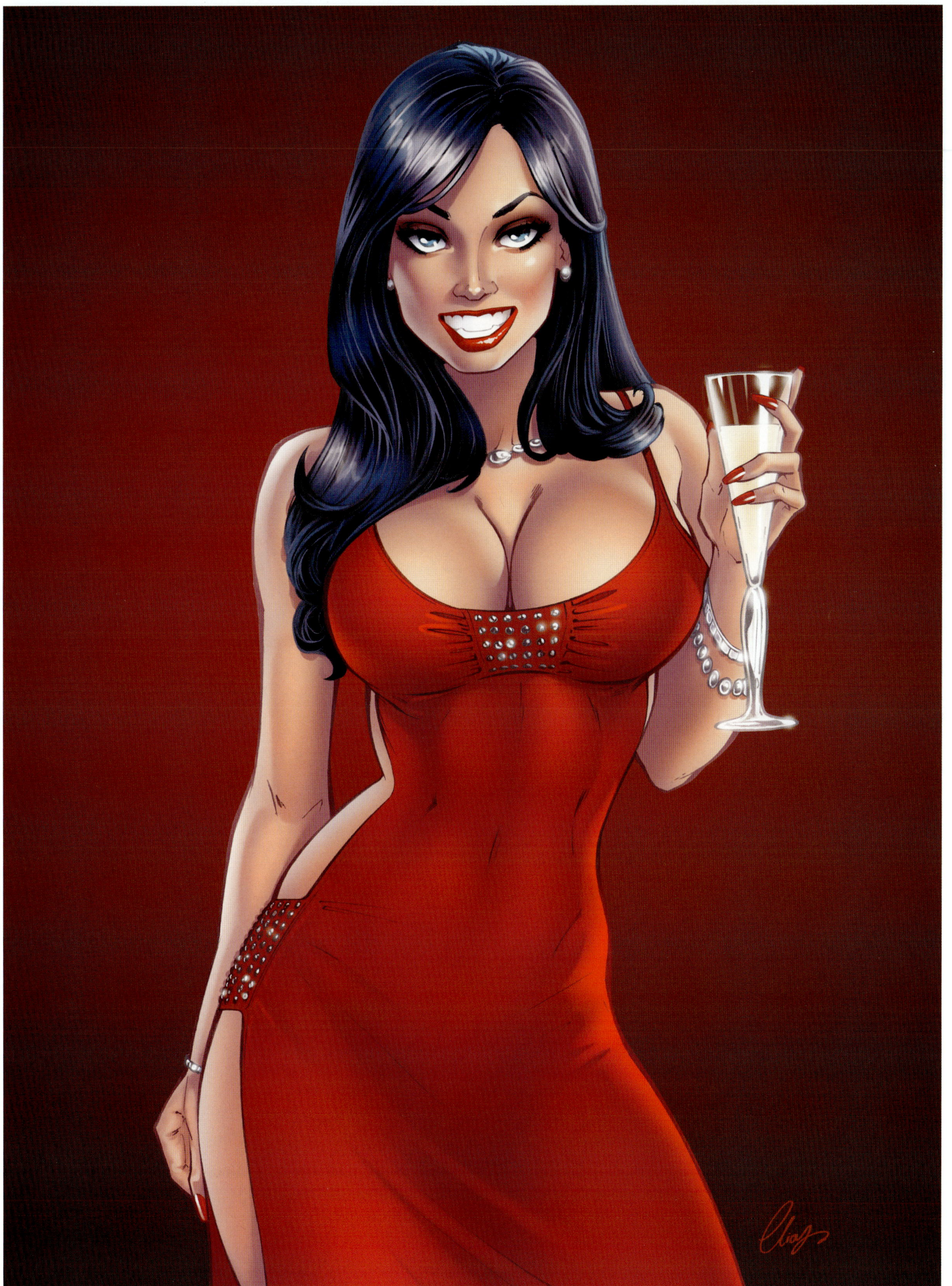

Cheers

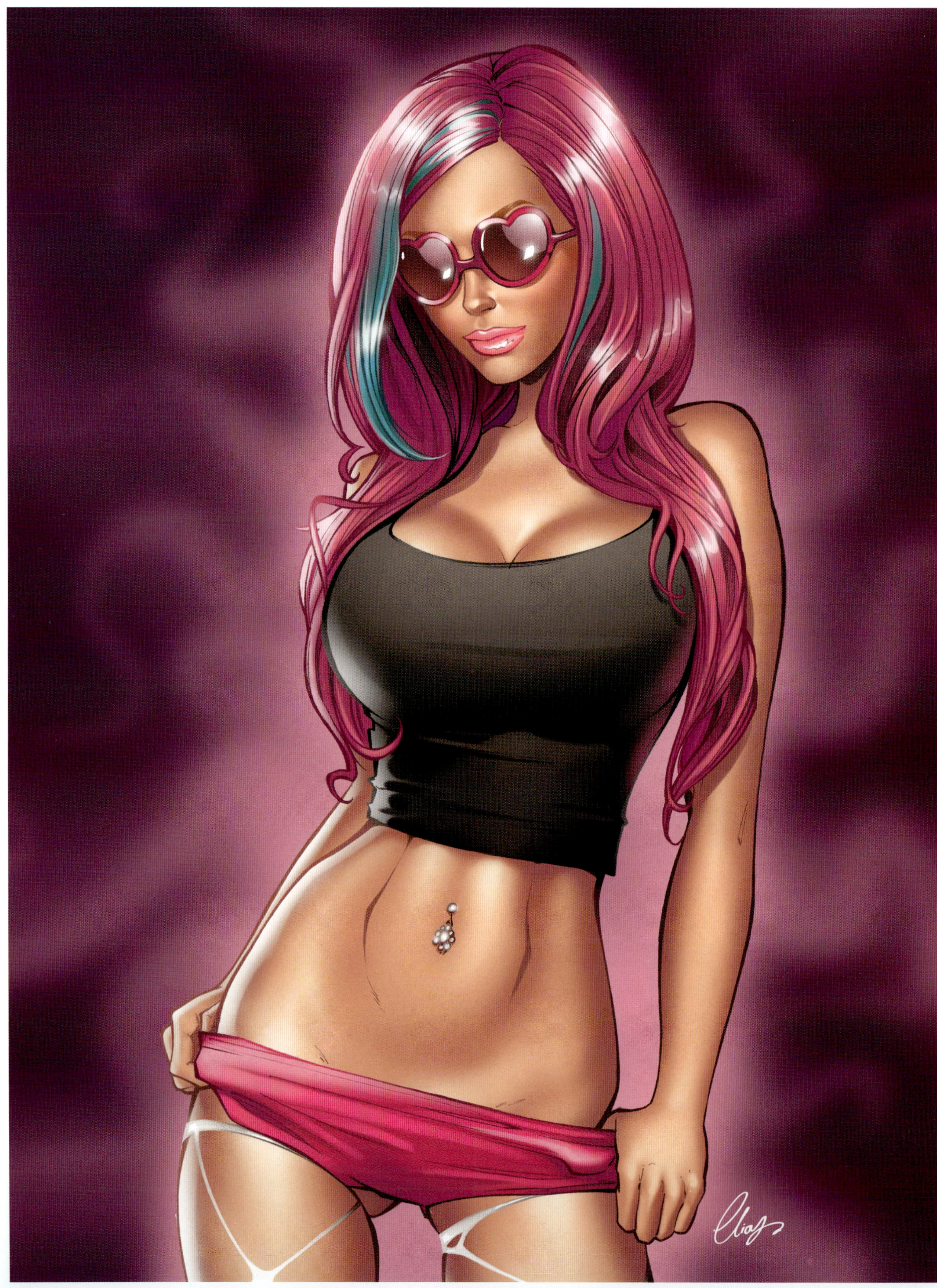

Pinky

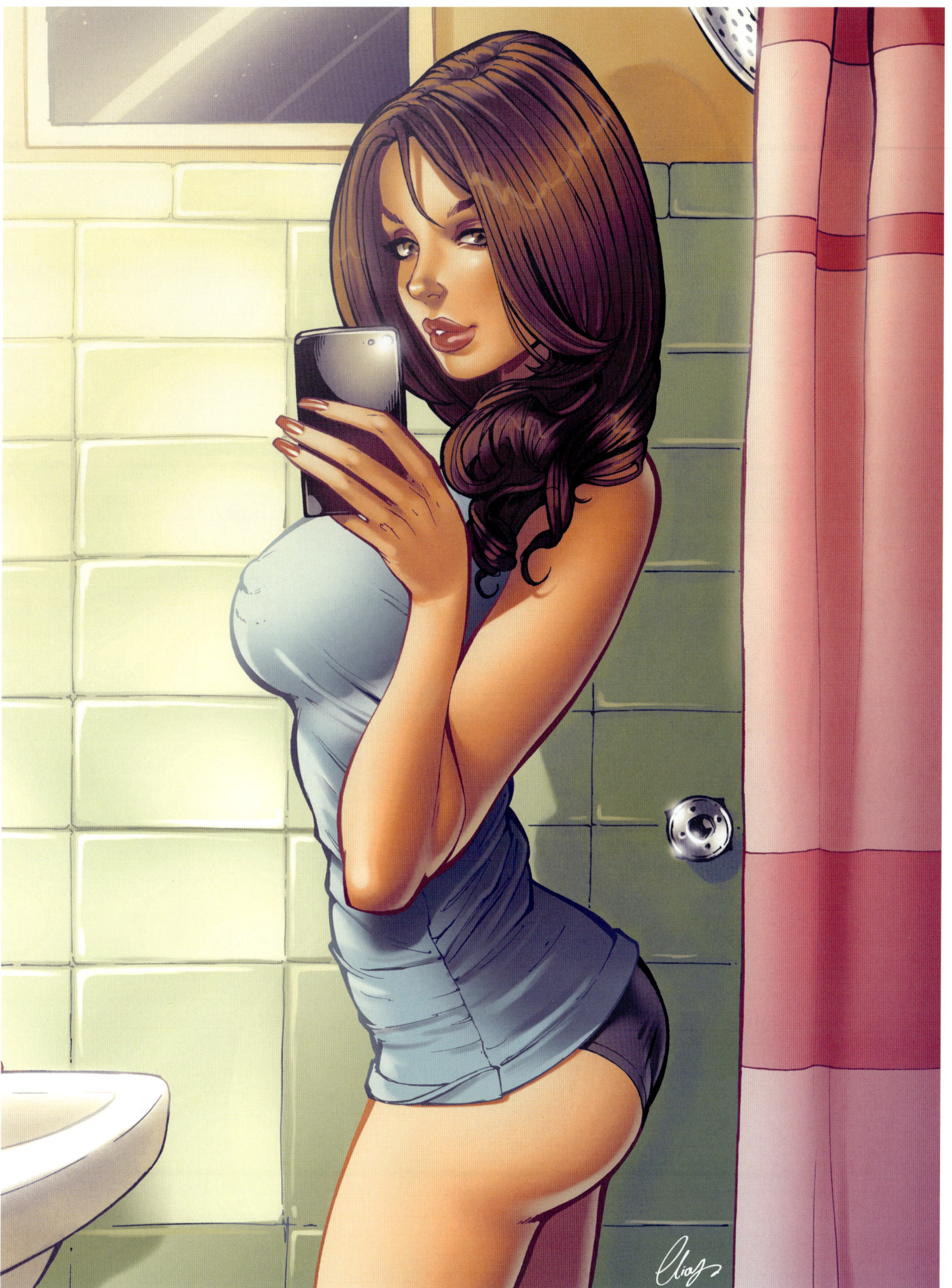

Sexting

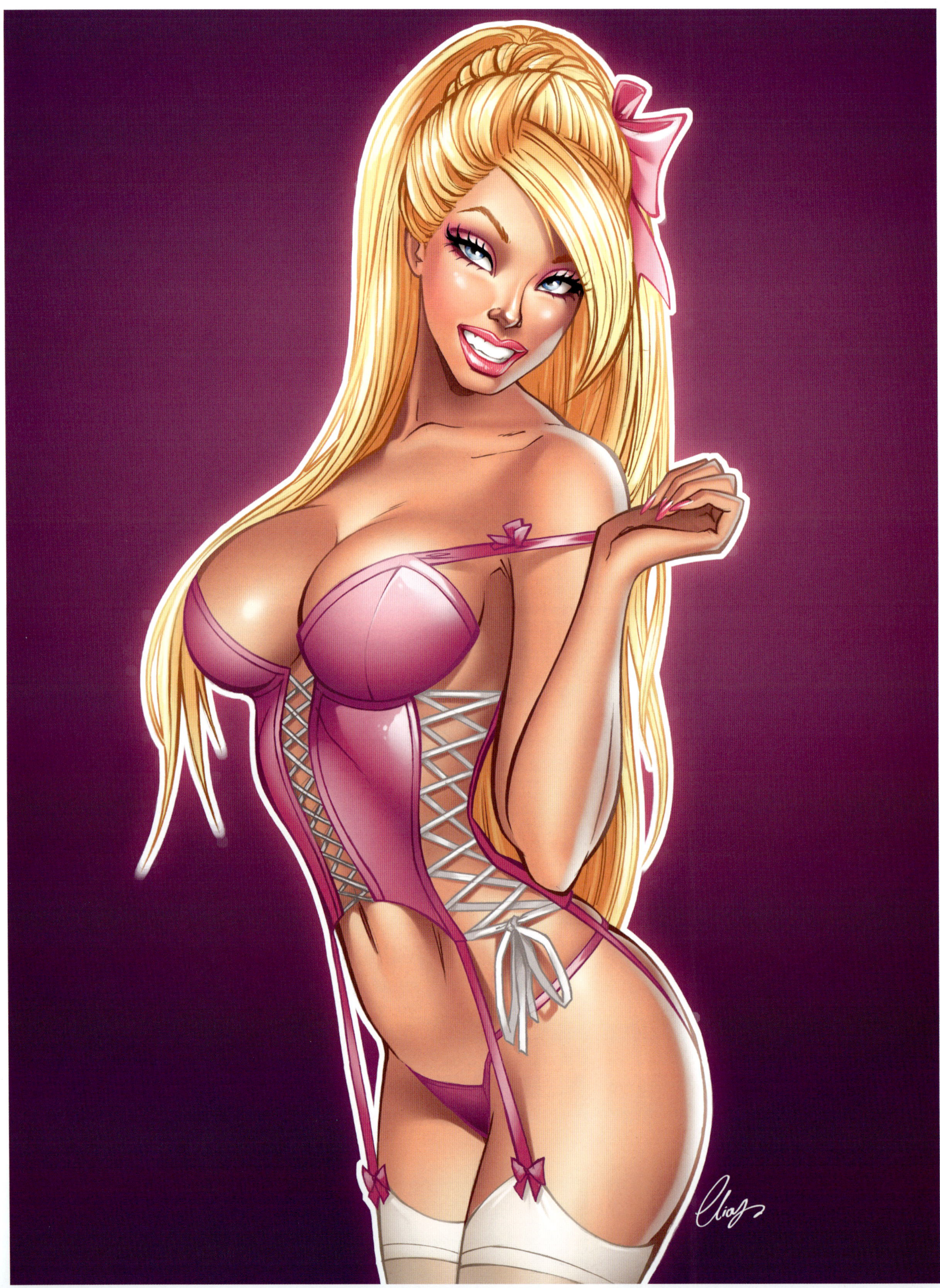

Plastic Is Fantastic

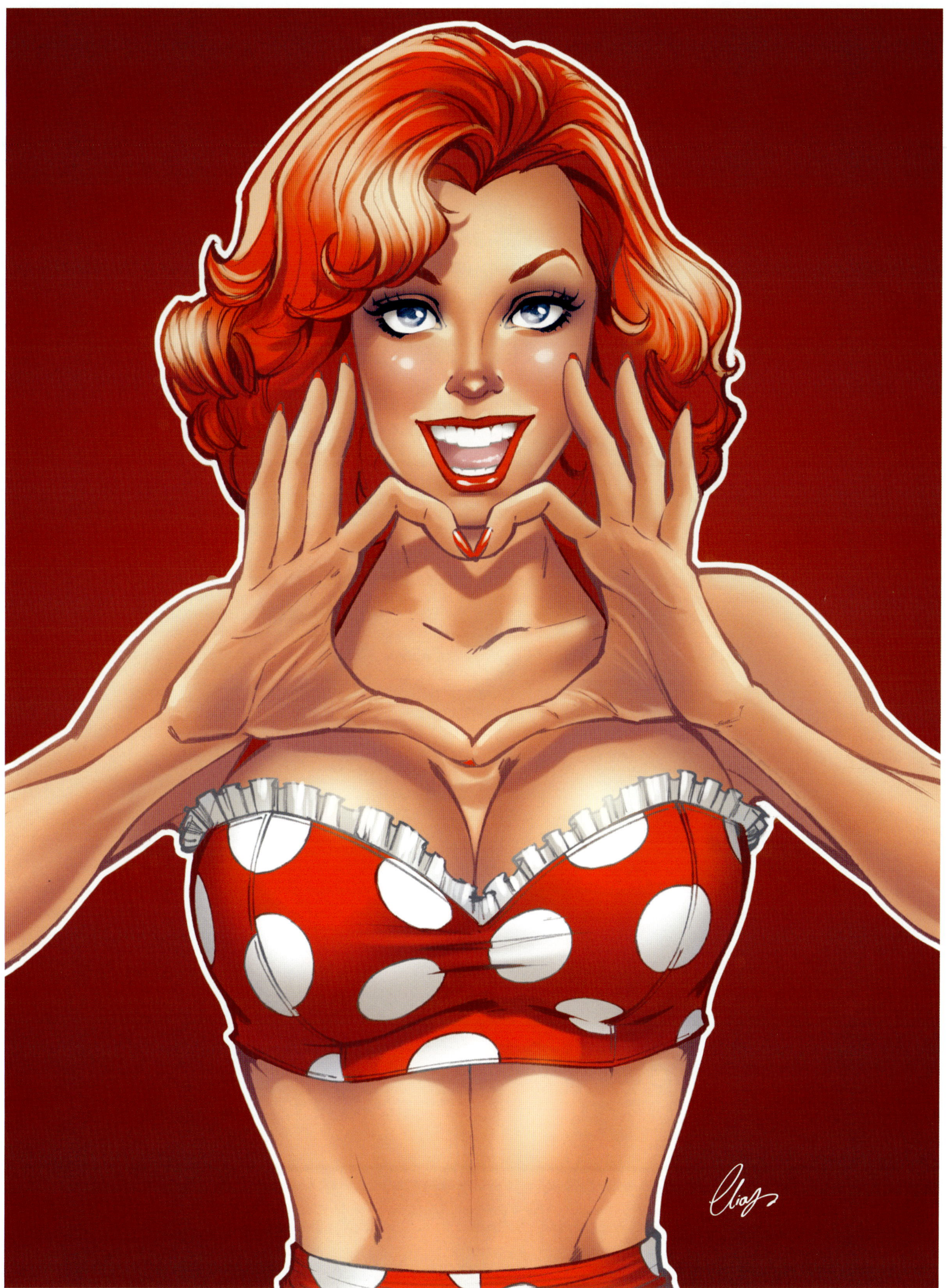

I Love U

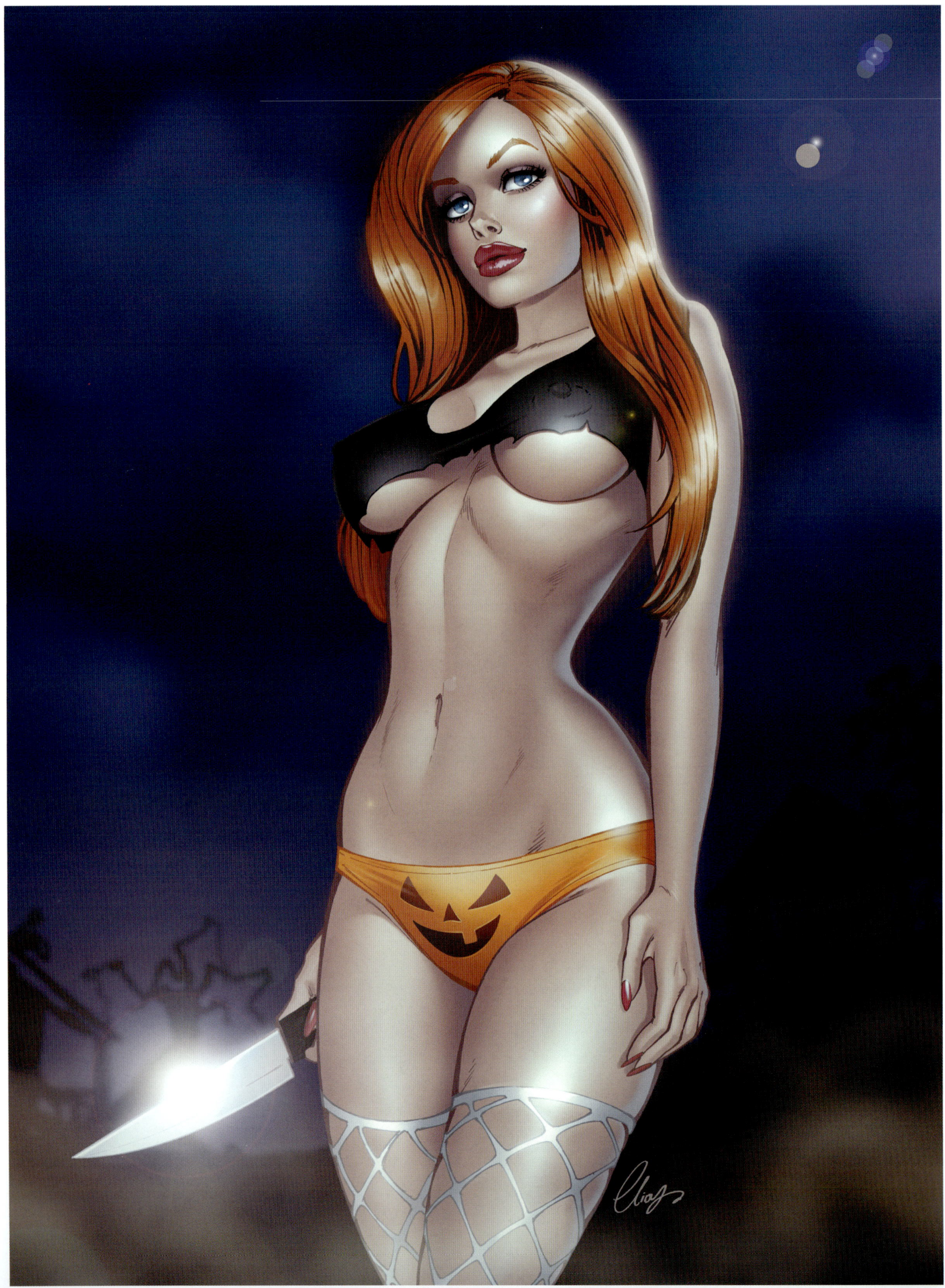

LOREINA

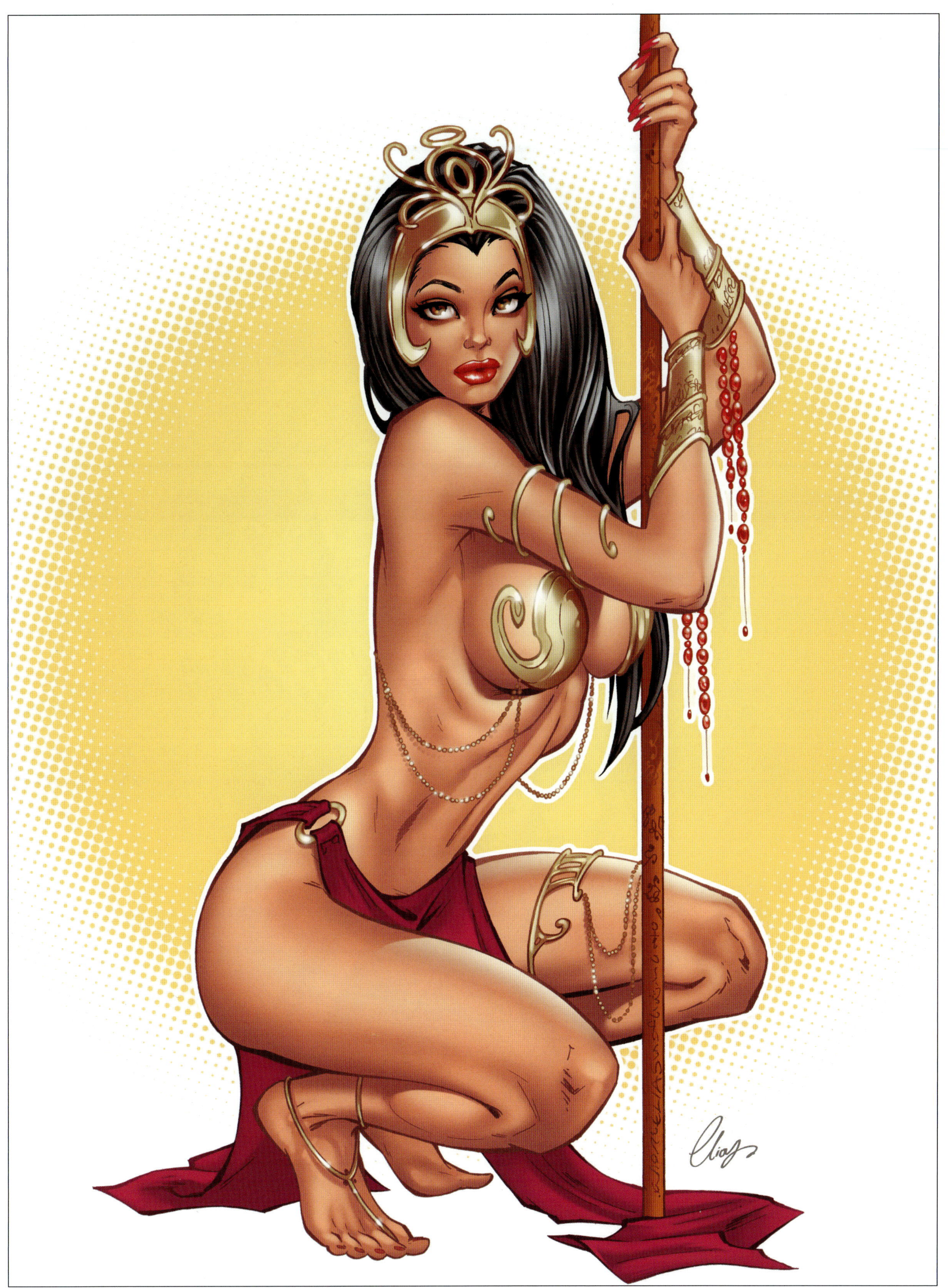

Denia

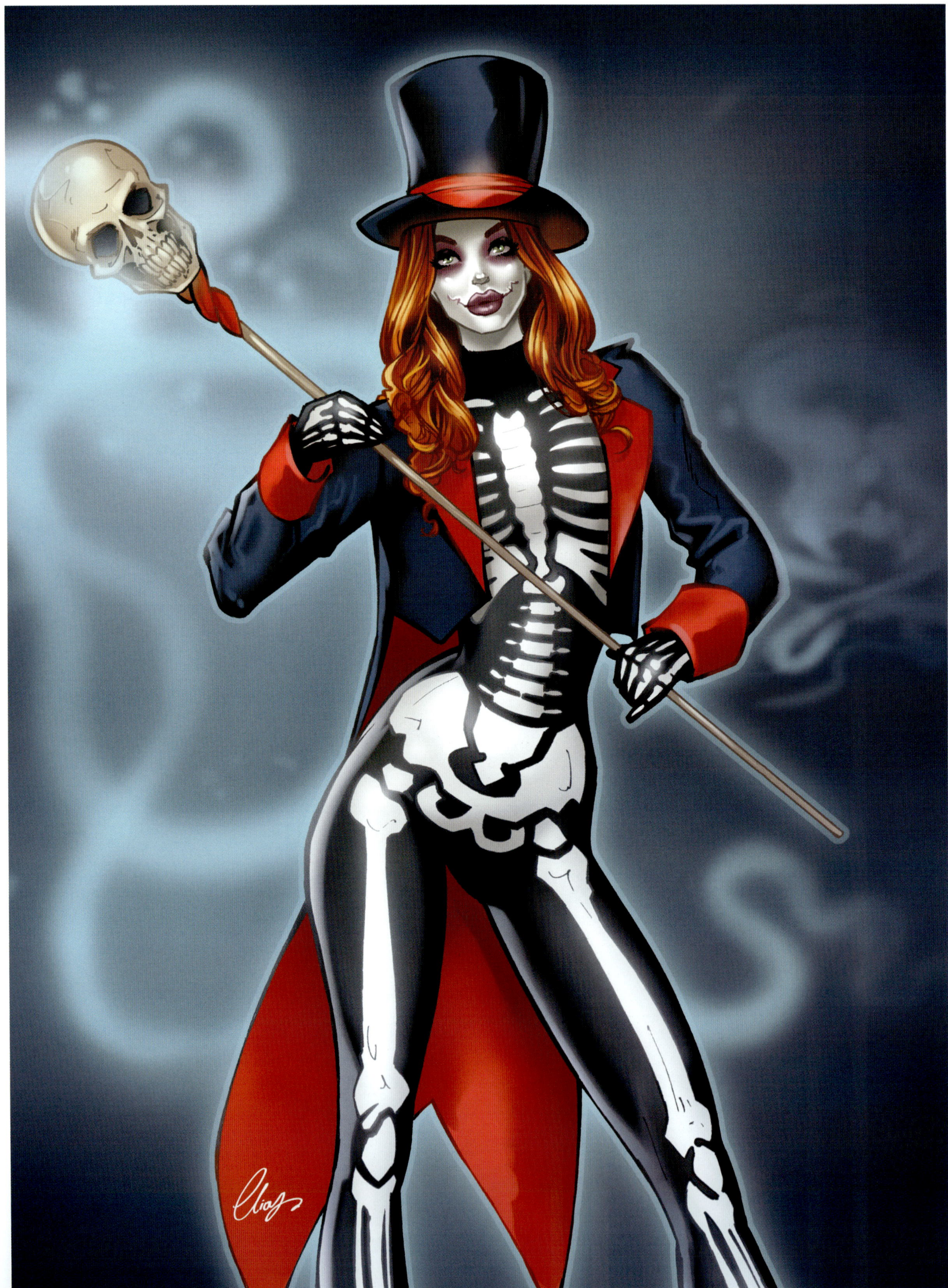

Ms. Voodoo

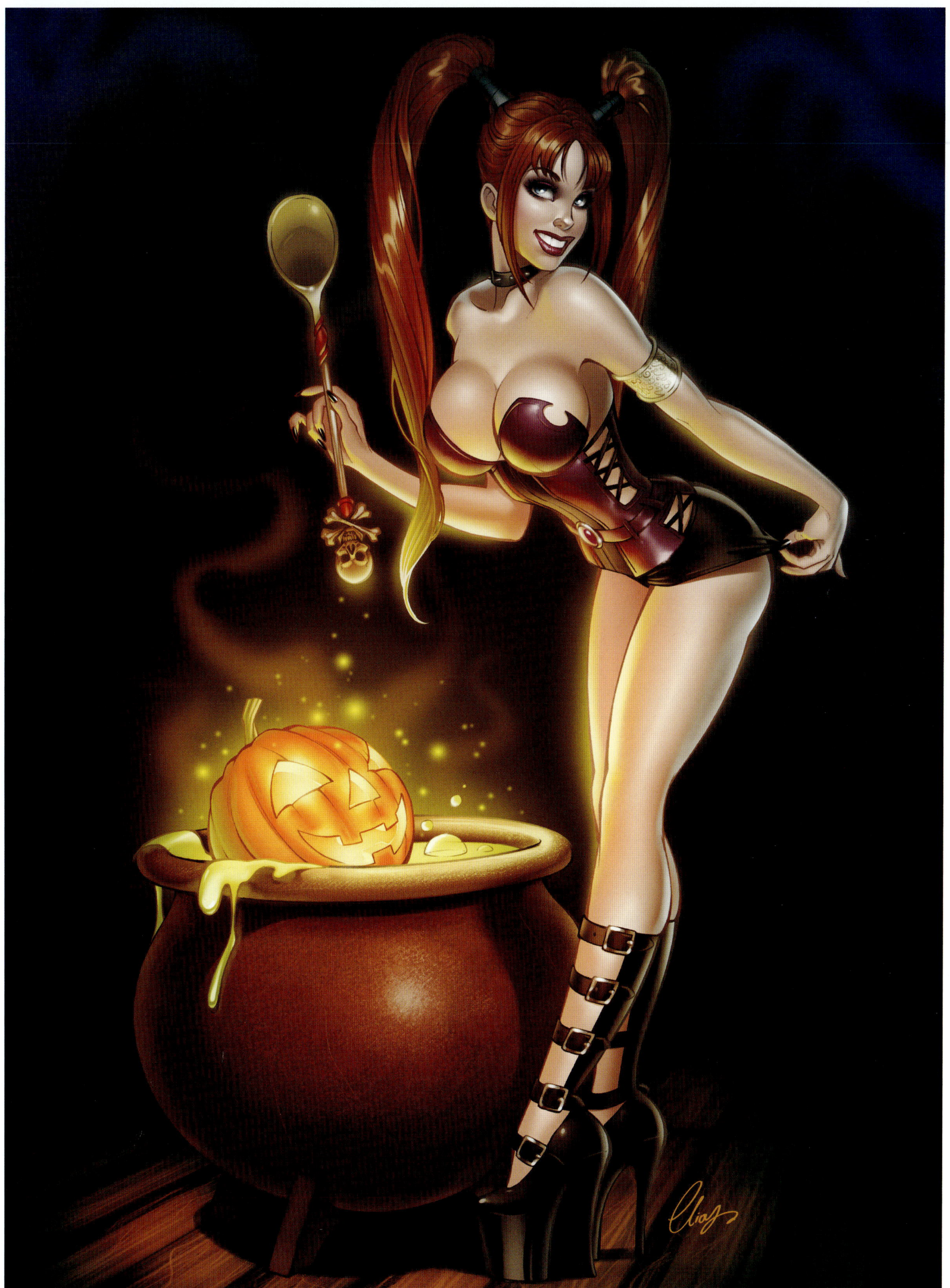

Hocus Pocus

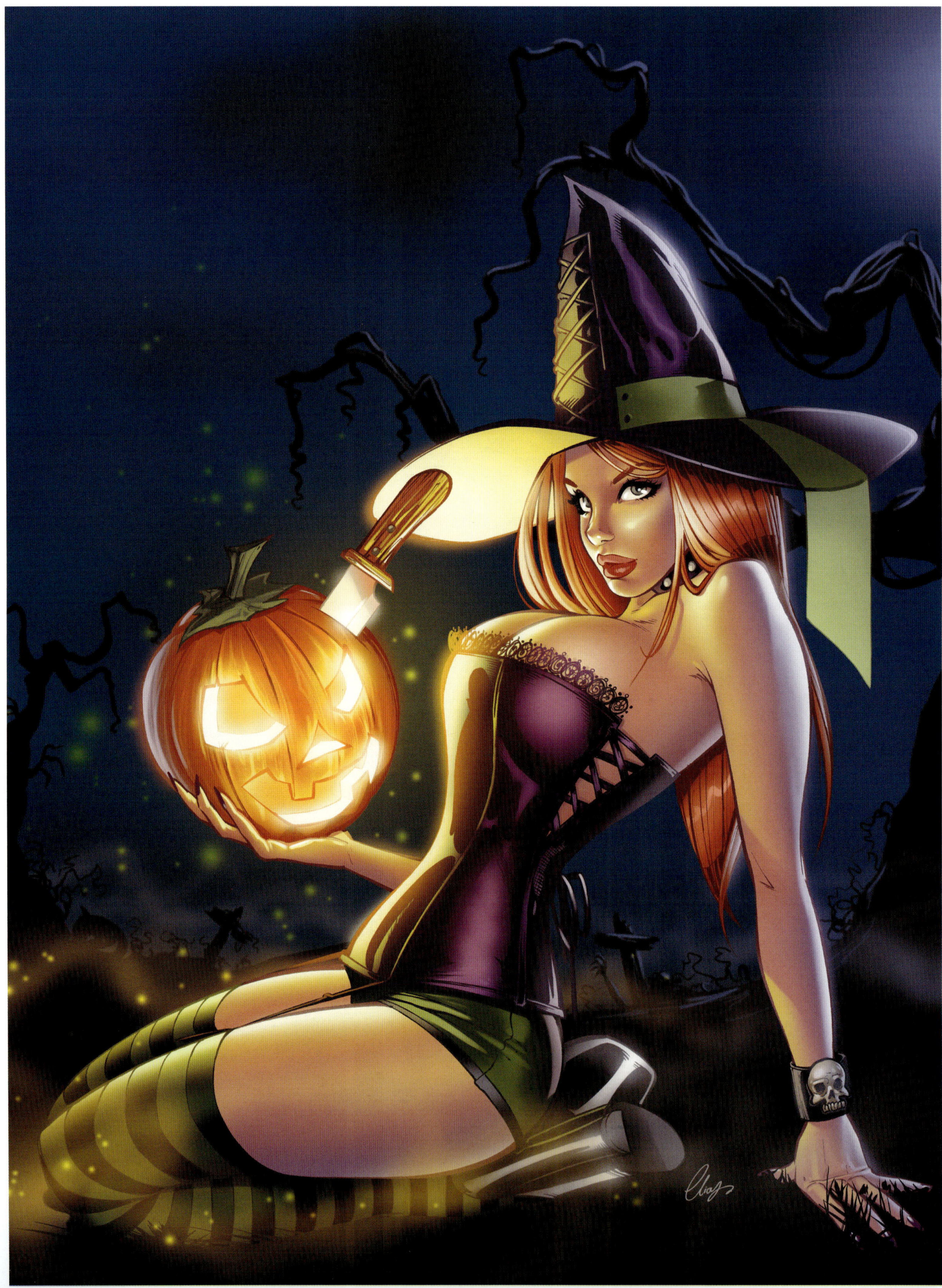

Magica

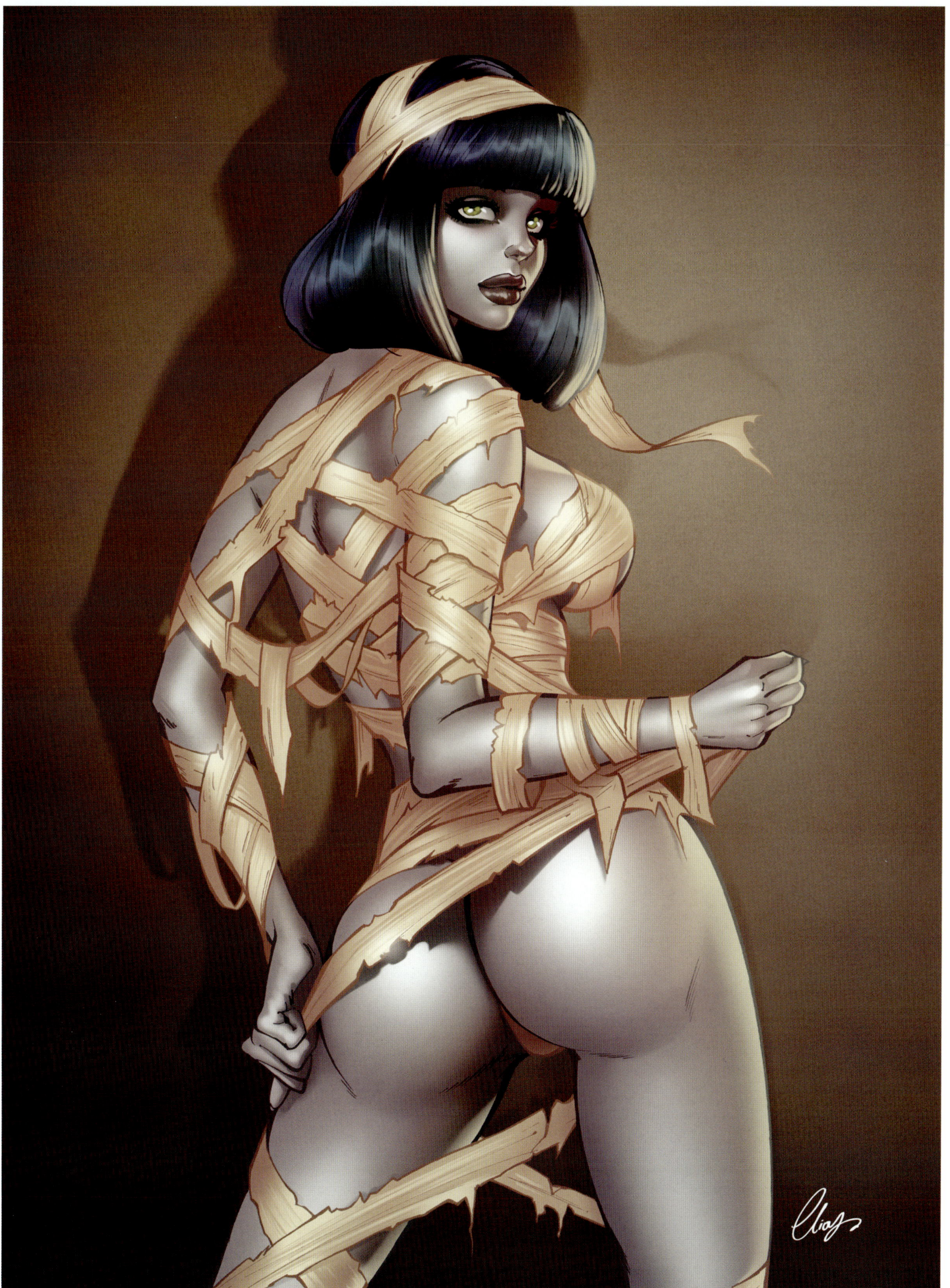

MUMMY MIA

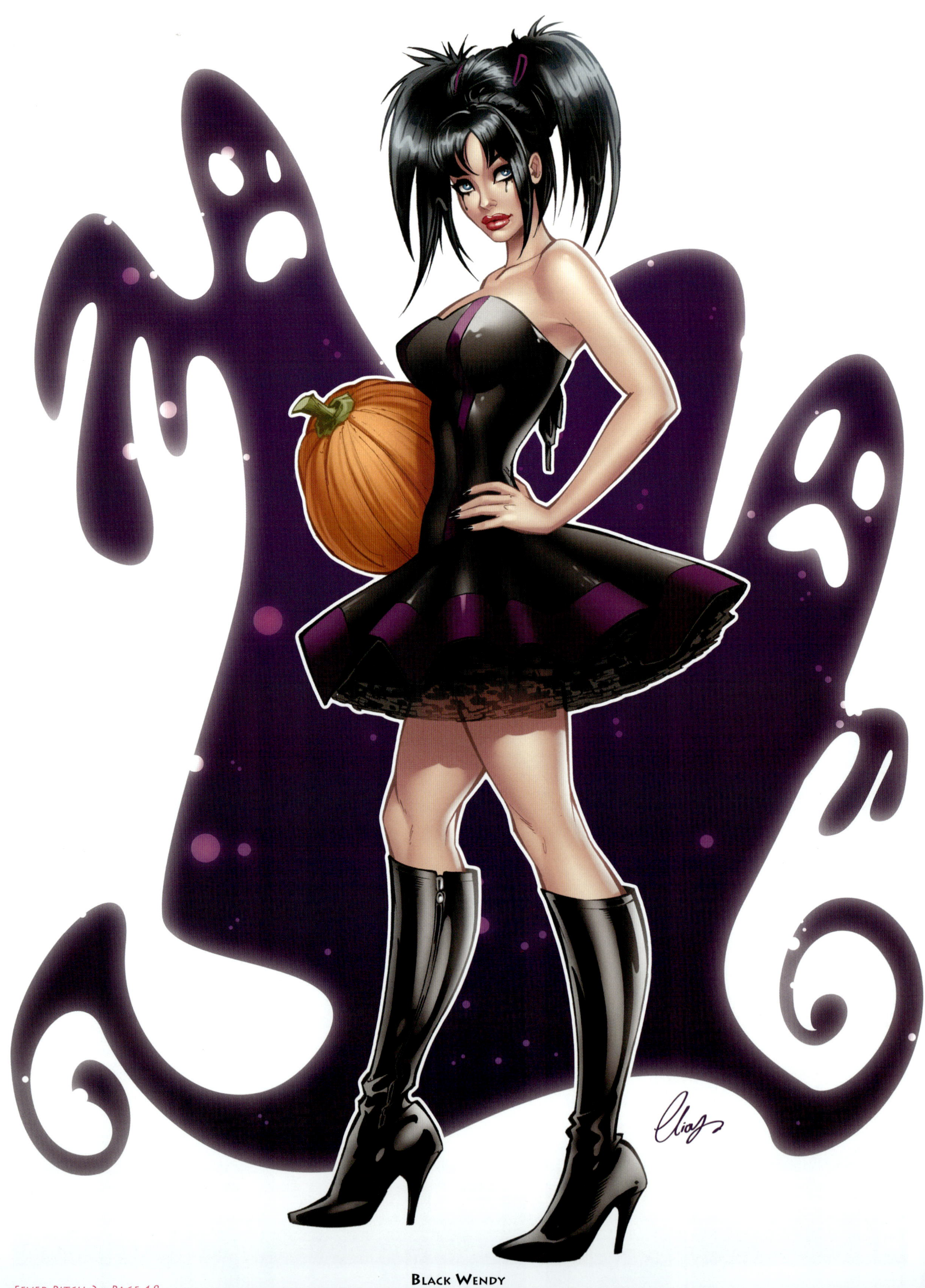

BLACK WENDY

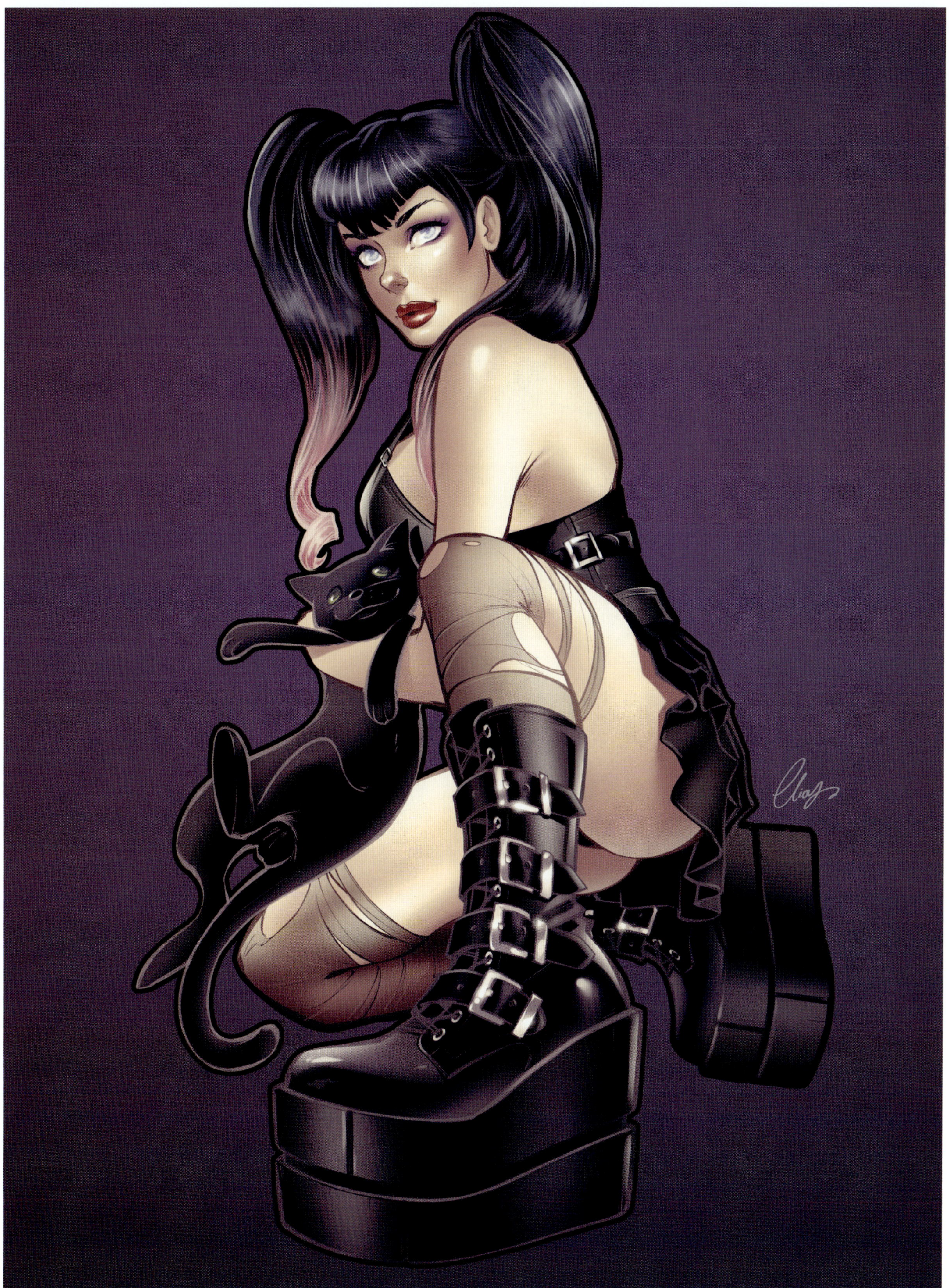

Eleonora

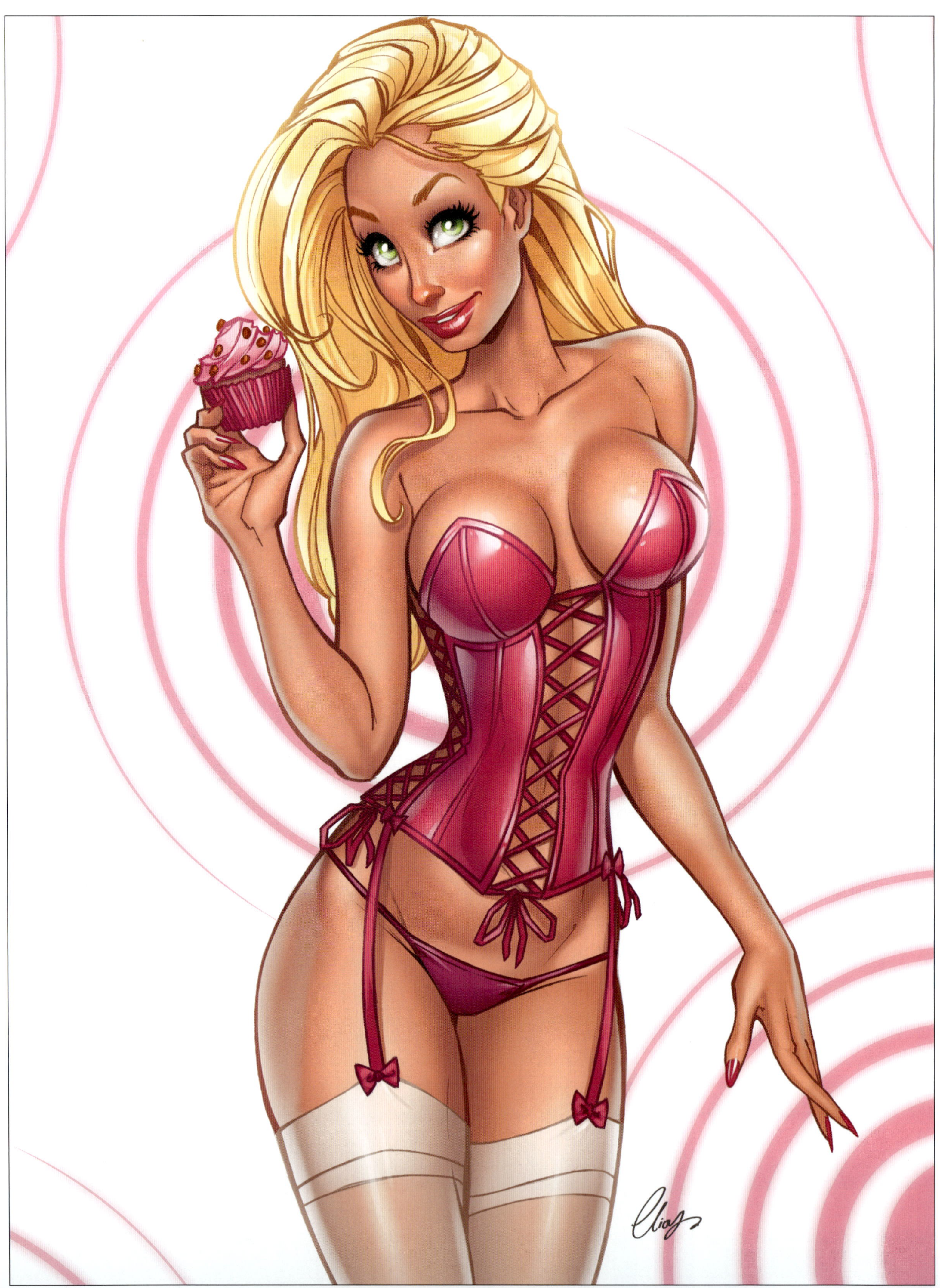

A Sweet Gift For You

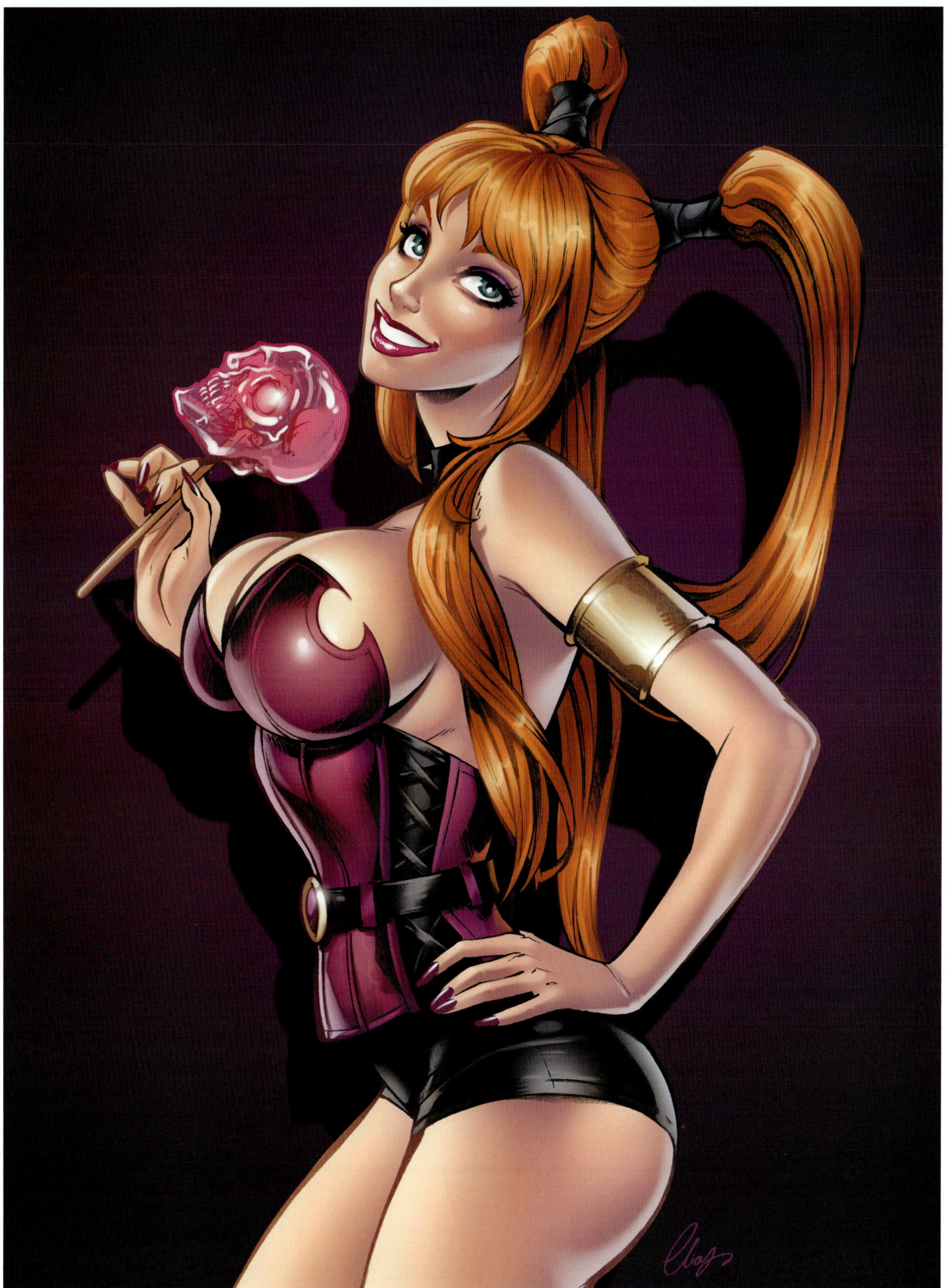

Cirke

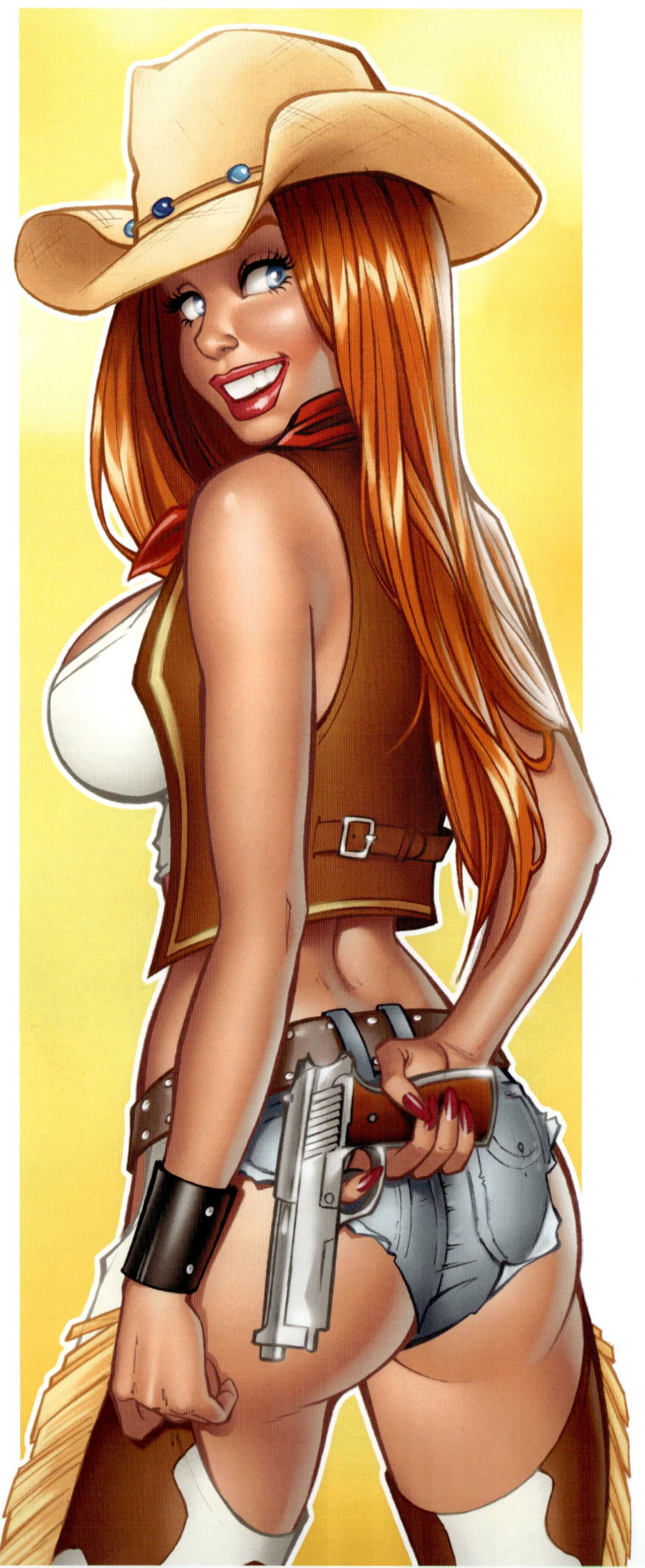

Daisy

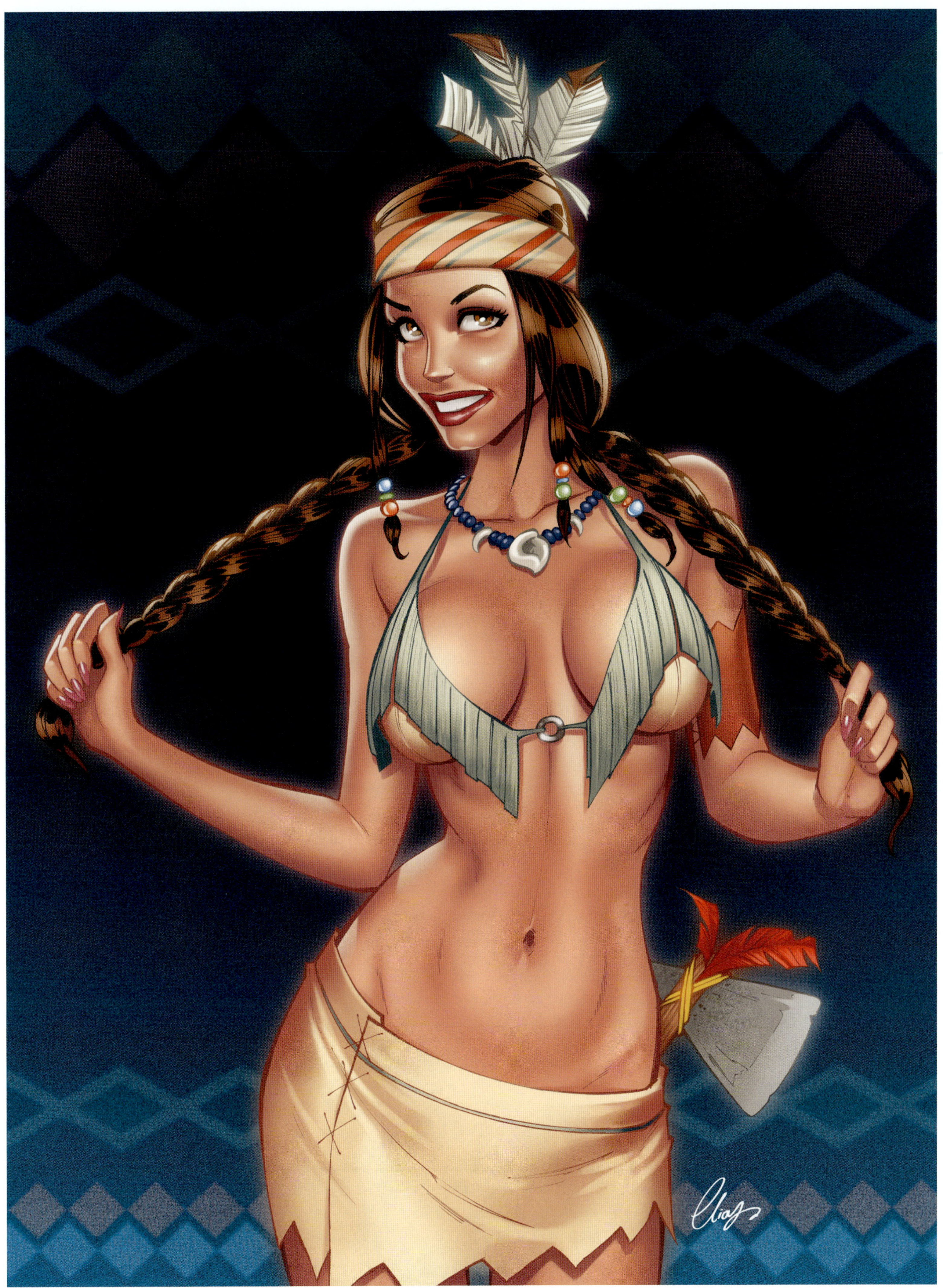

HAPPY INDIAN CHICK

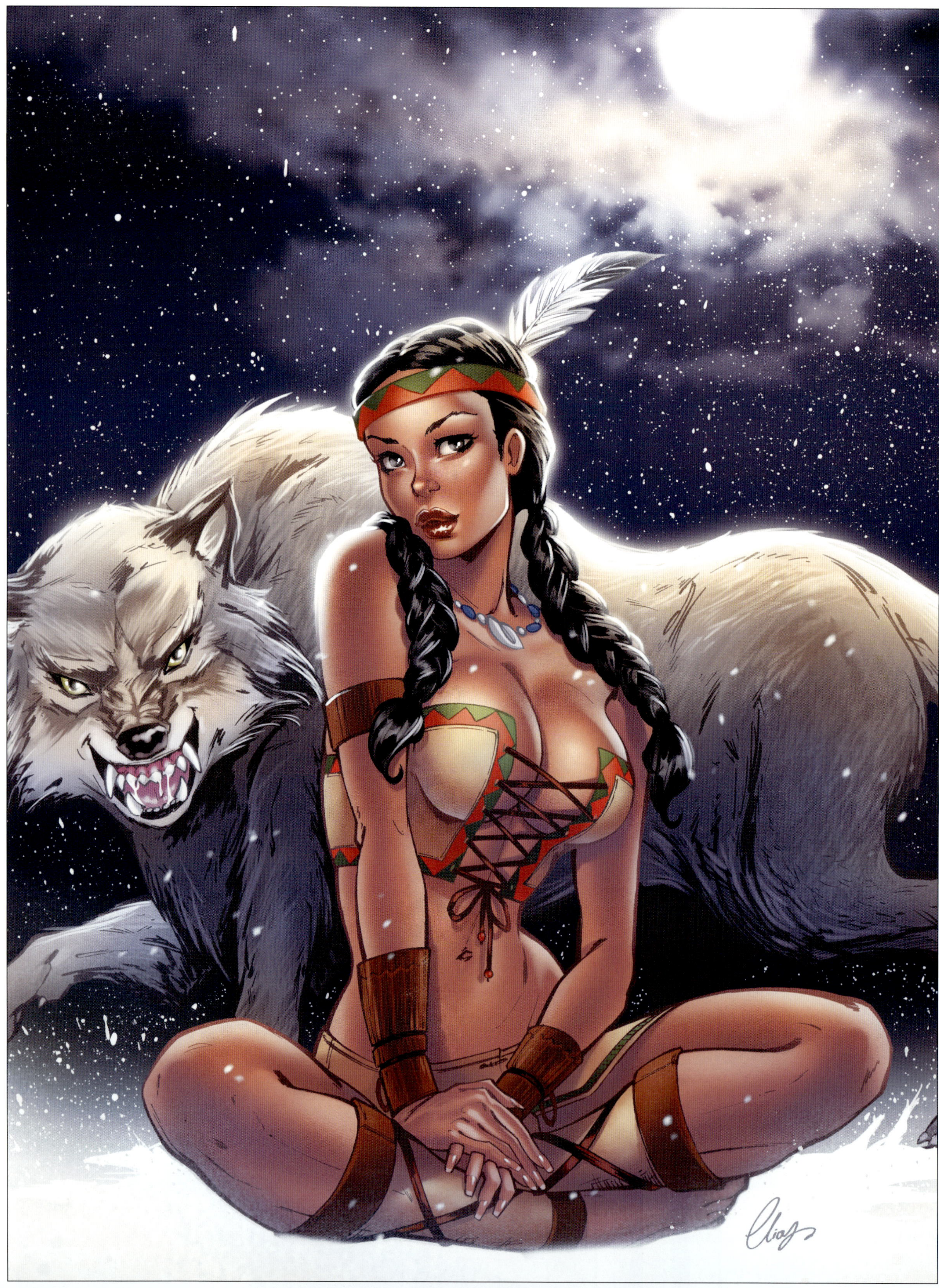

With Her Pet

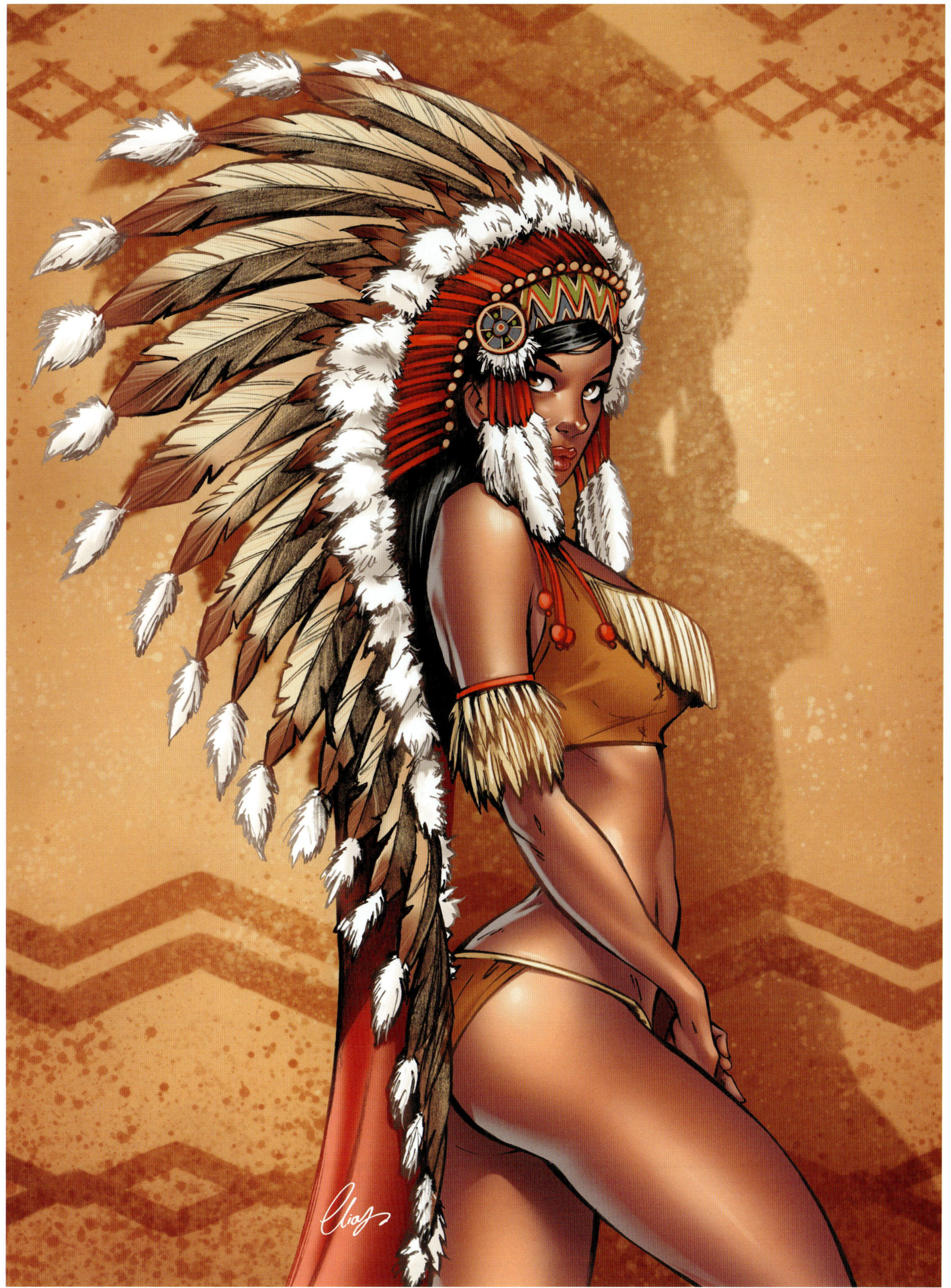

Ciquala

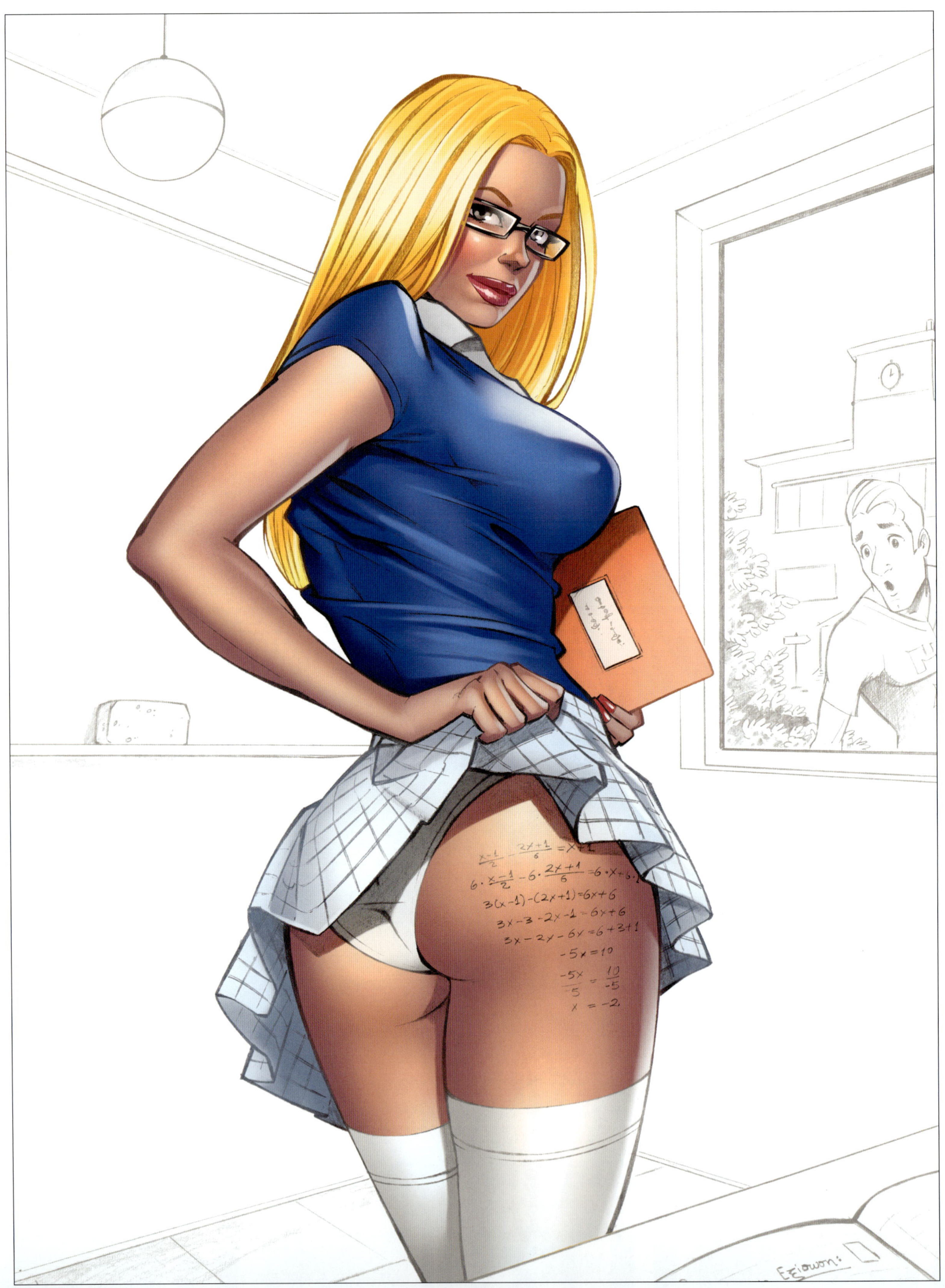

$\frac{x-1}{2} - \frac{2x+1}{6} = x+1$
$6 \cdot \frac{x-1}{2} - 6 \cdot \frac{2x+1}{6} = 6 \cdot x + 6 \cdot 1$
$3(x-1) - (2x+1) = 6x+6$
$3x - 3 - 2x - 1 = 6x + 6$
$3x - 2x - 6x = 6 + 3 + 1$
$-5x = 10$
$\frac{-5x}{-5} = \frac{10}{-5}$
$x = -2$

CHEAT SHEET

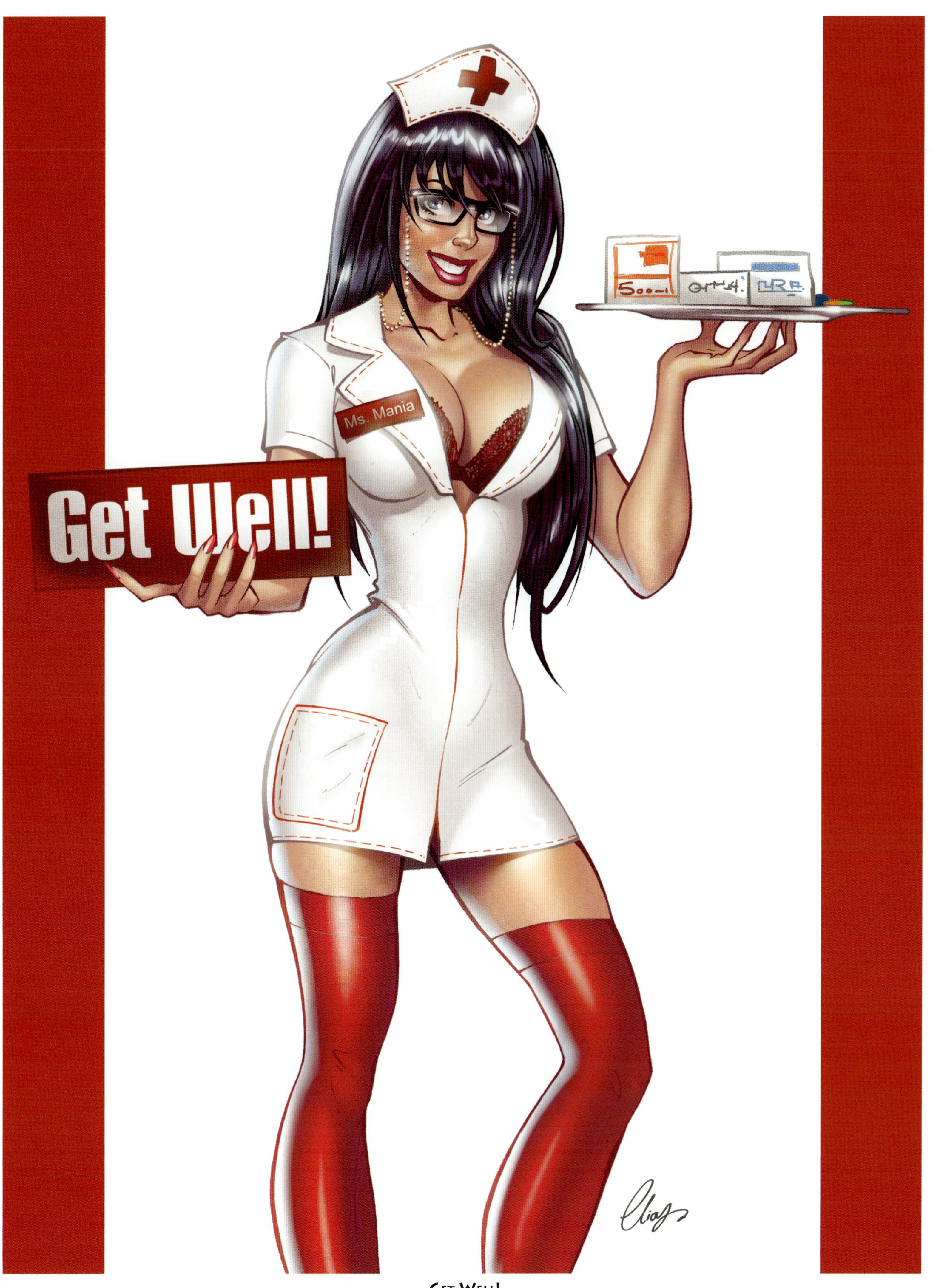

Ms. Mania
Get Well!

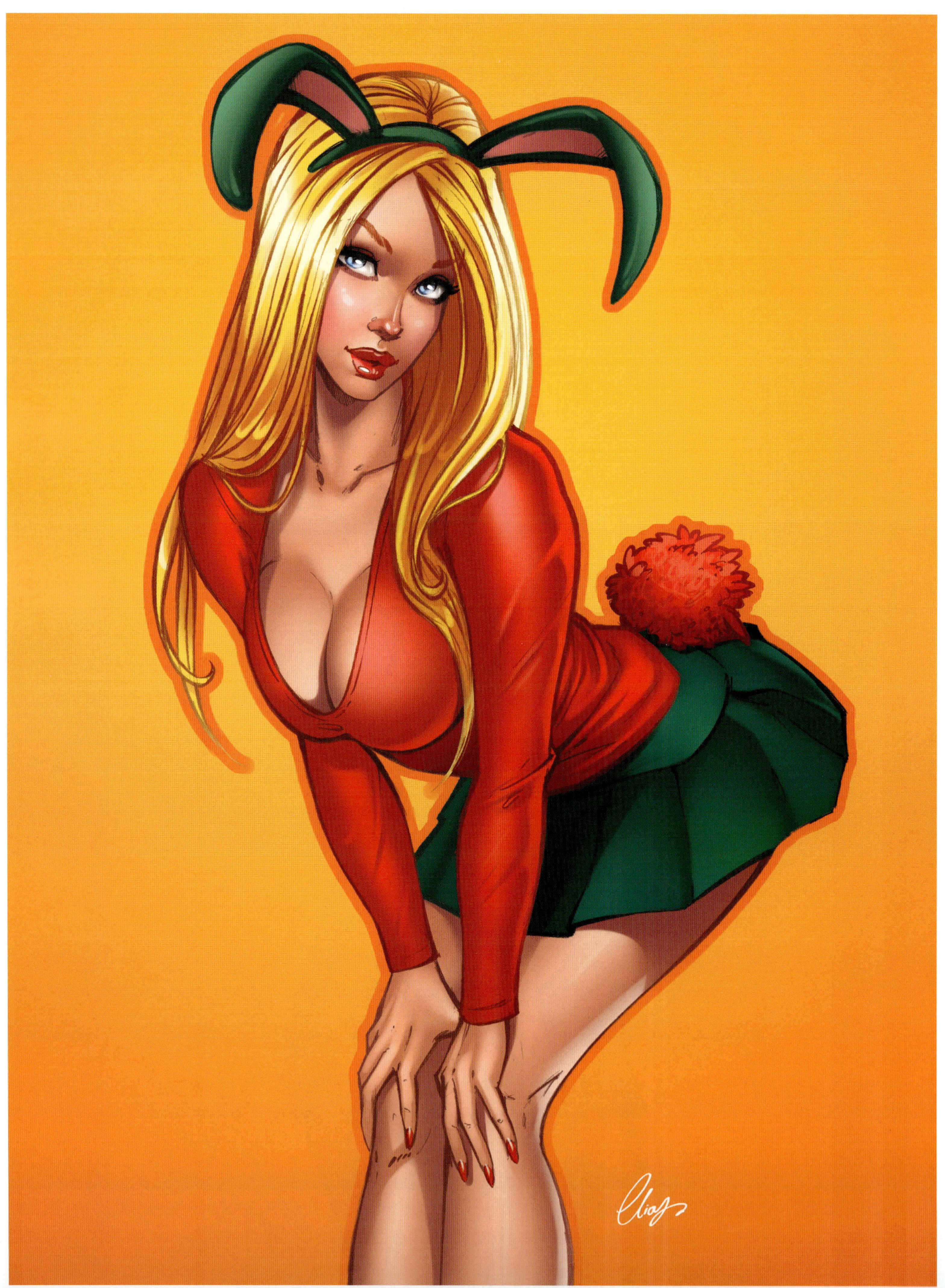

EASTER BUNNY

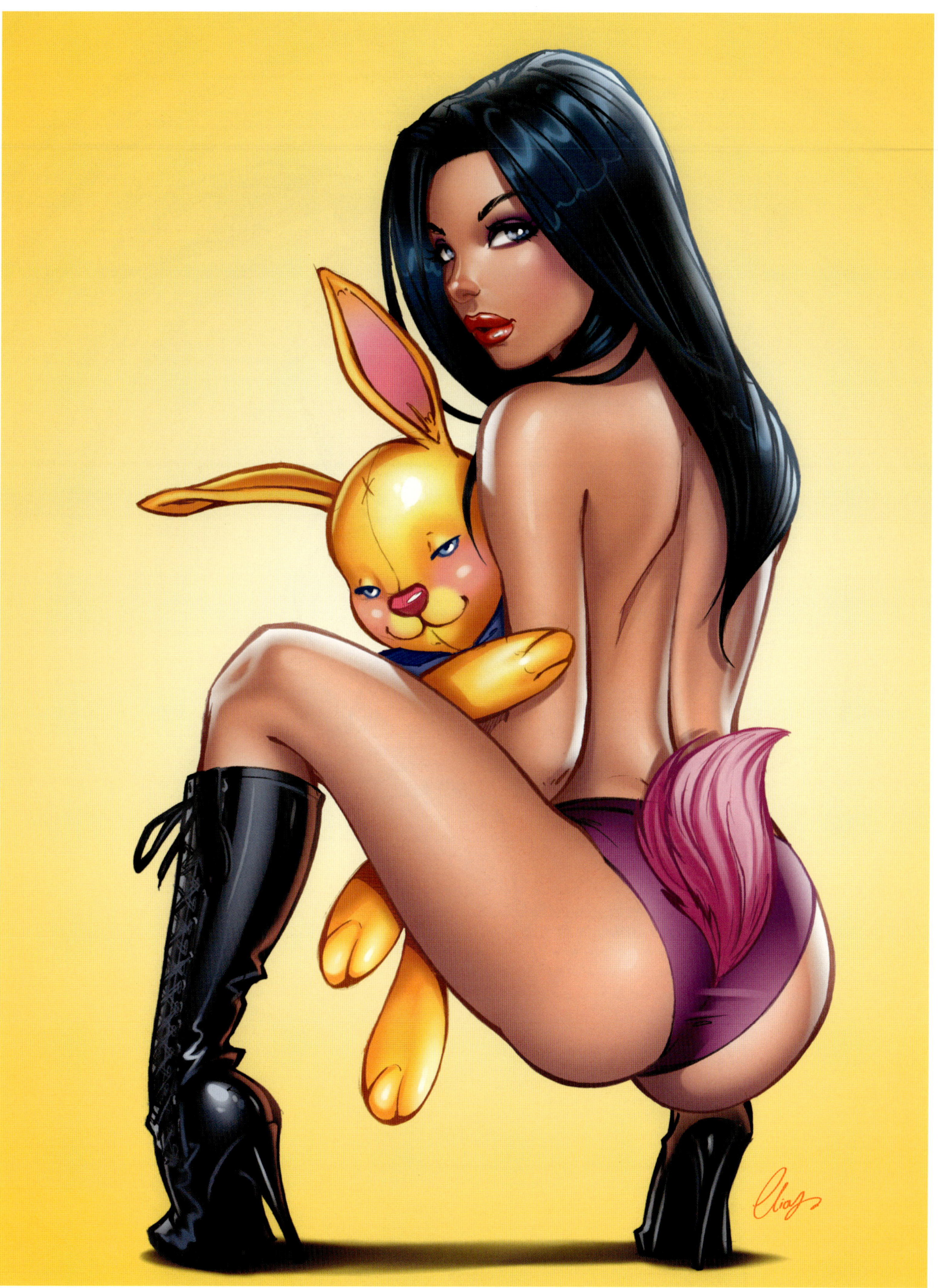

Honey Bunny

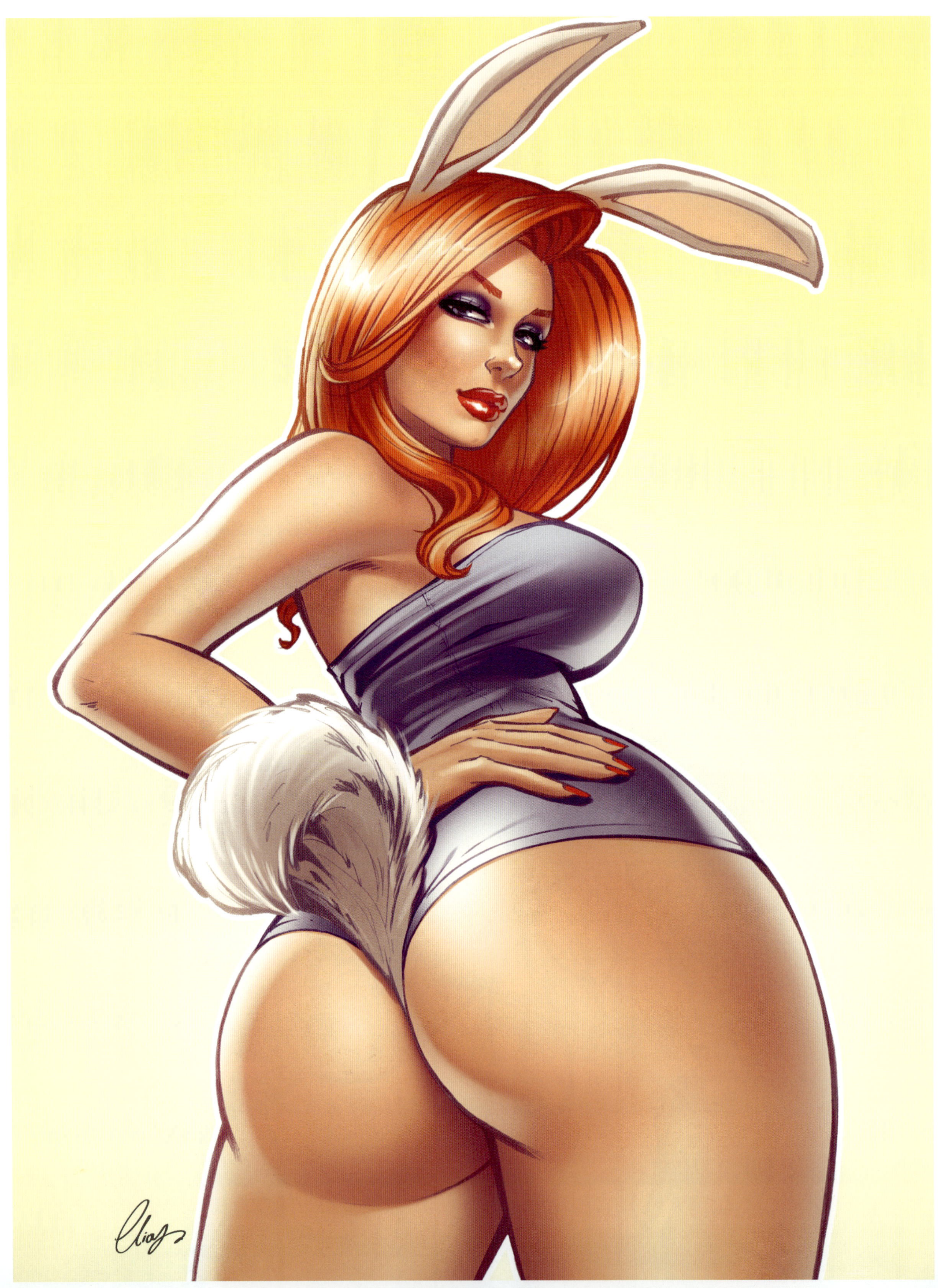

Super Sexy Bunny

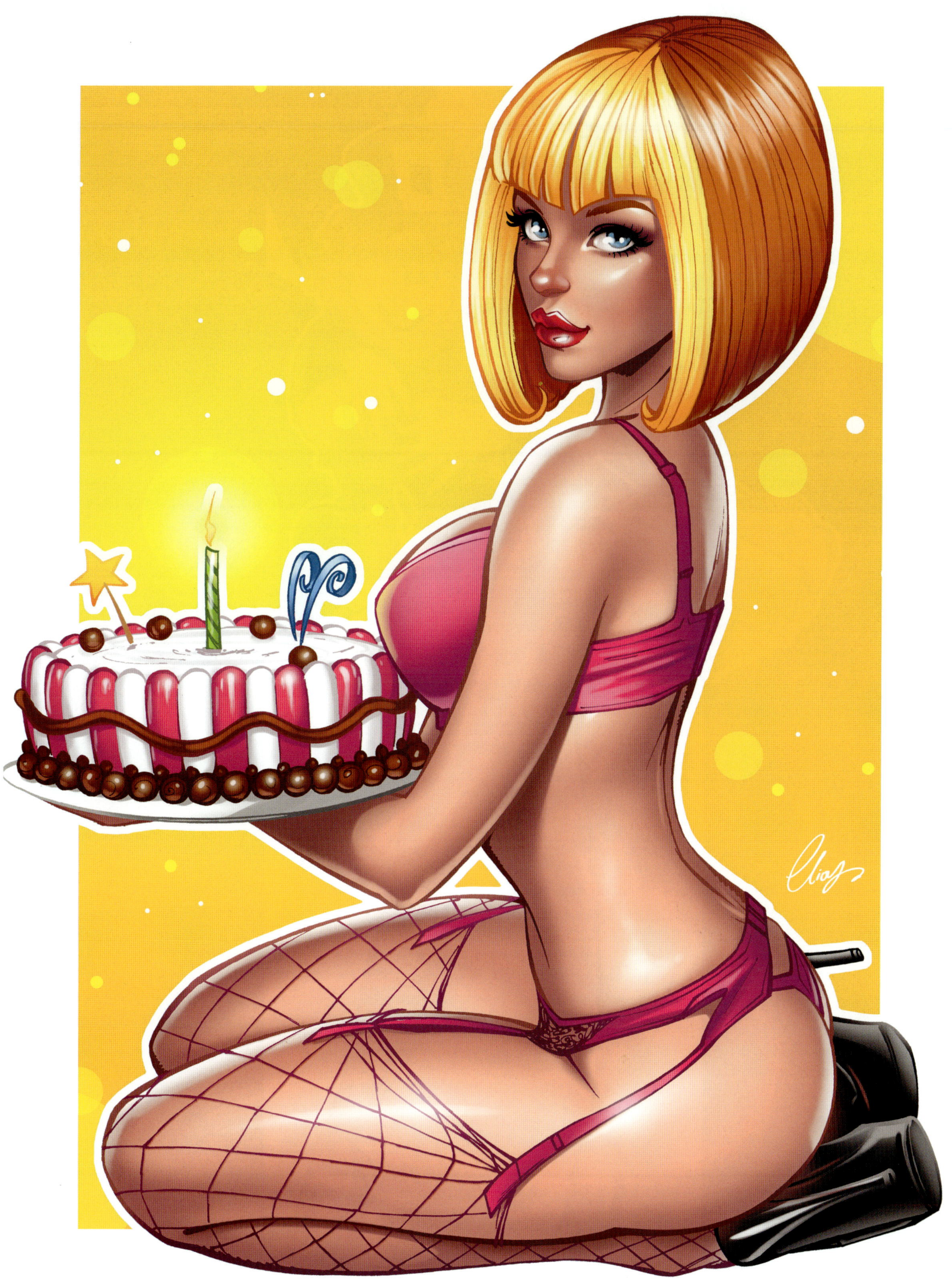

HAPPY BIRTHDAY

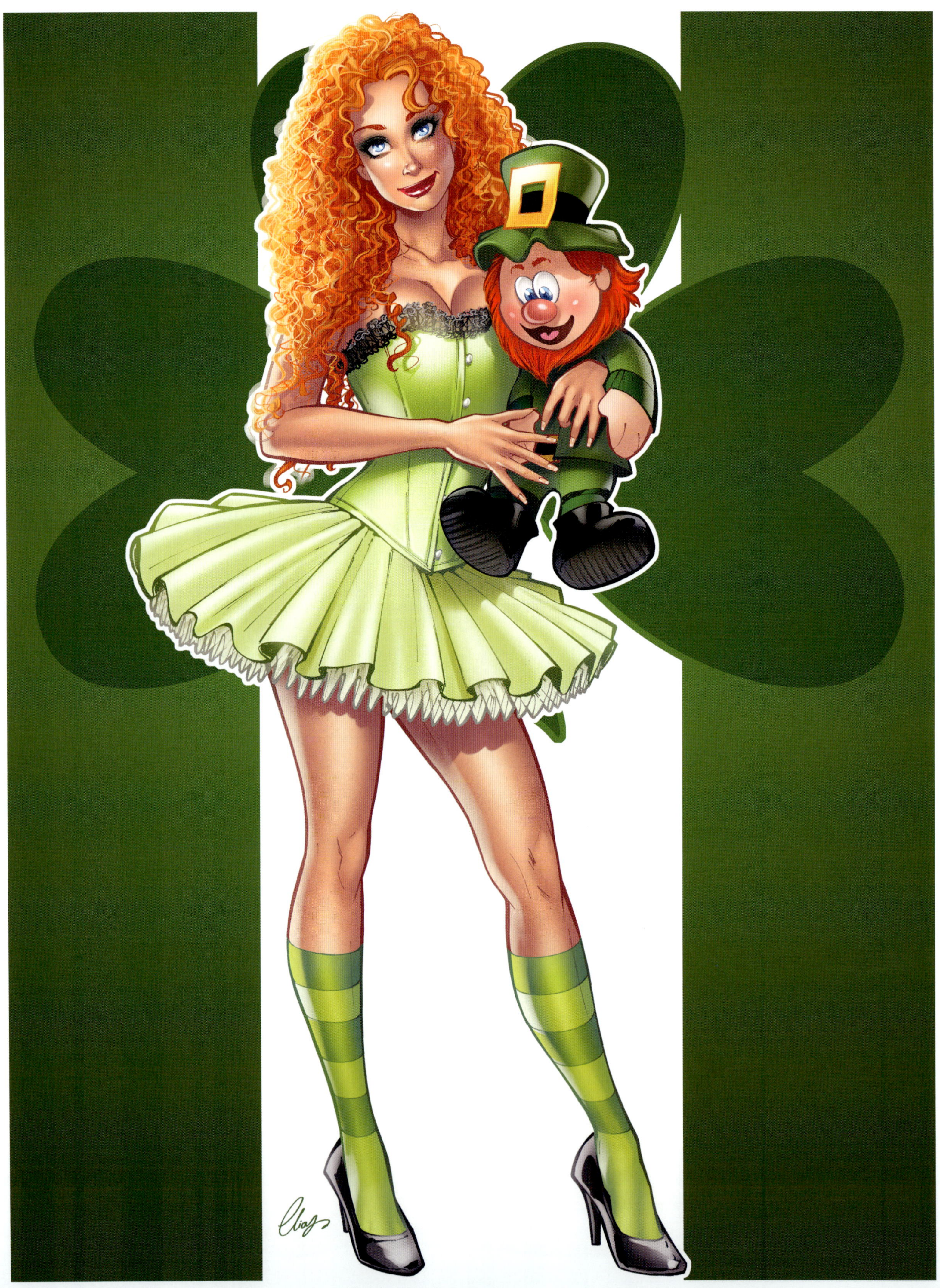

Sexy Patty

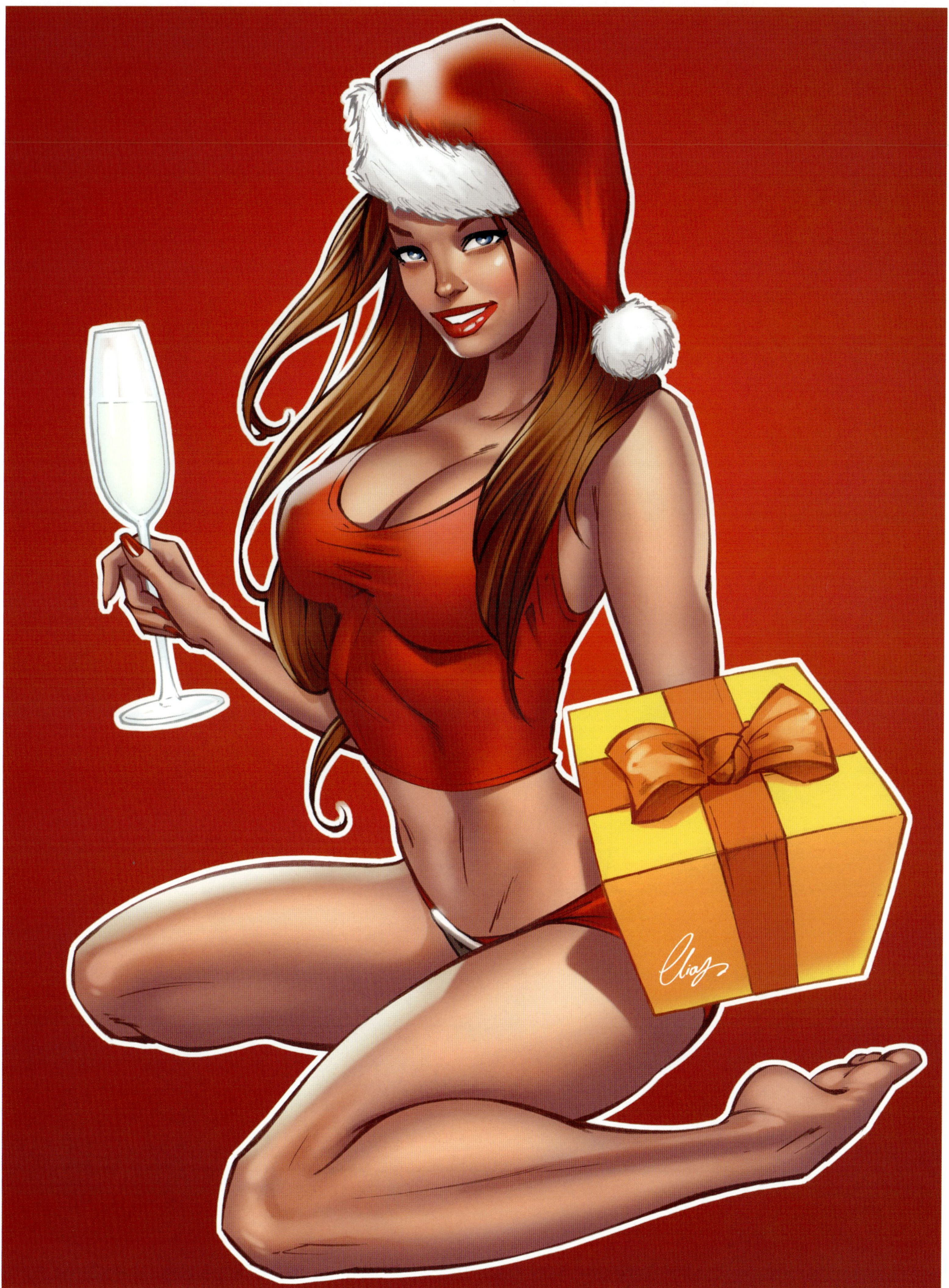

Unwrap Your Gifts

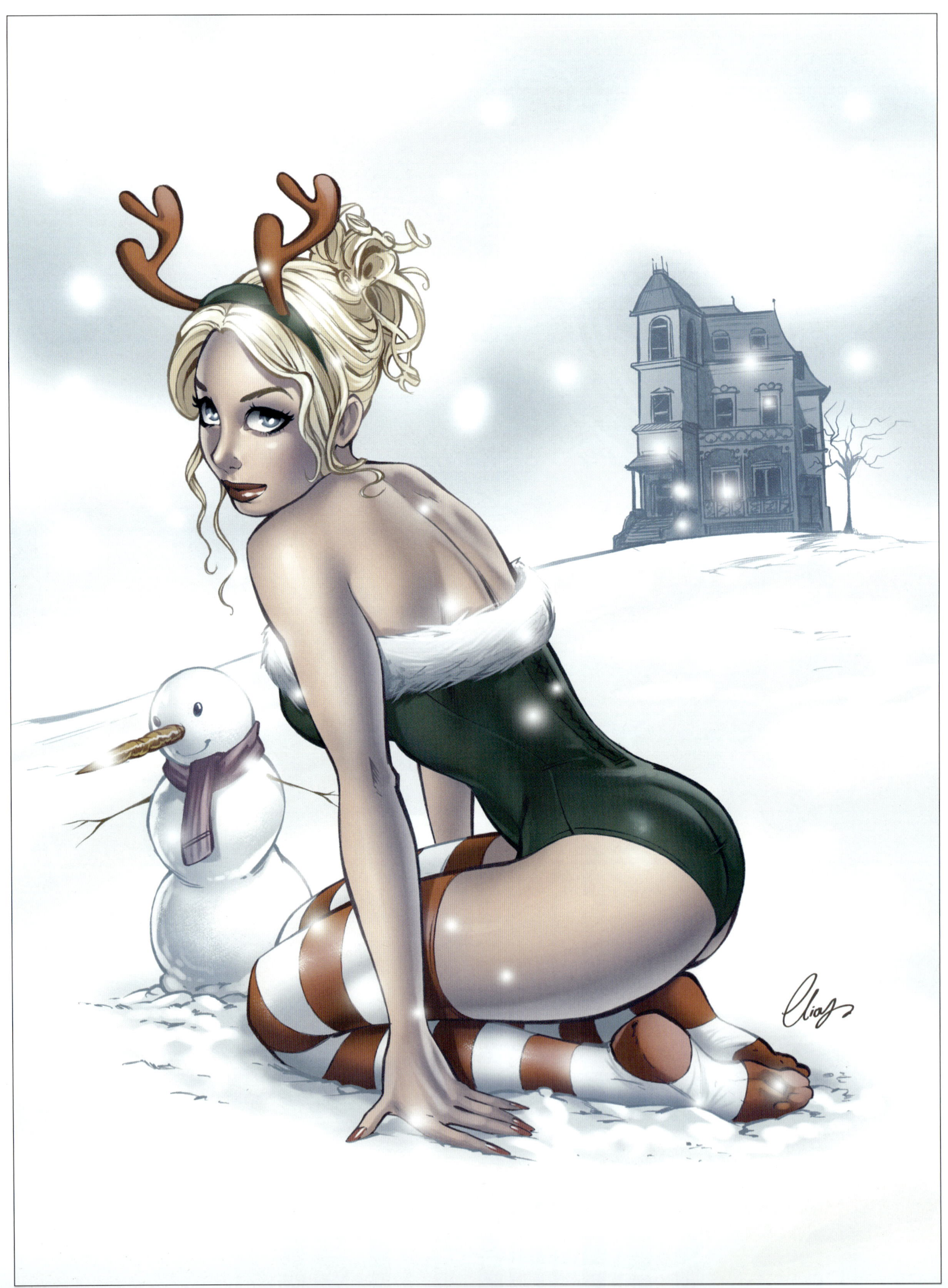

DEER HEART

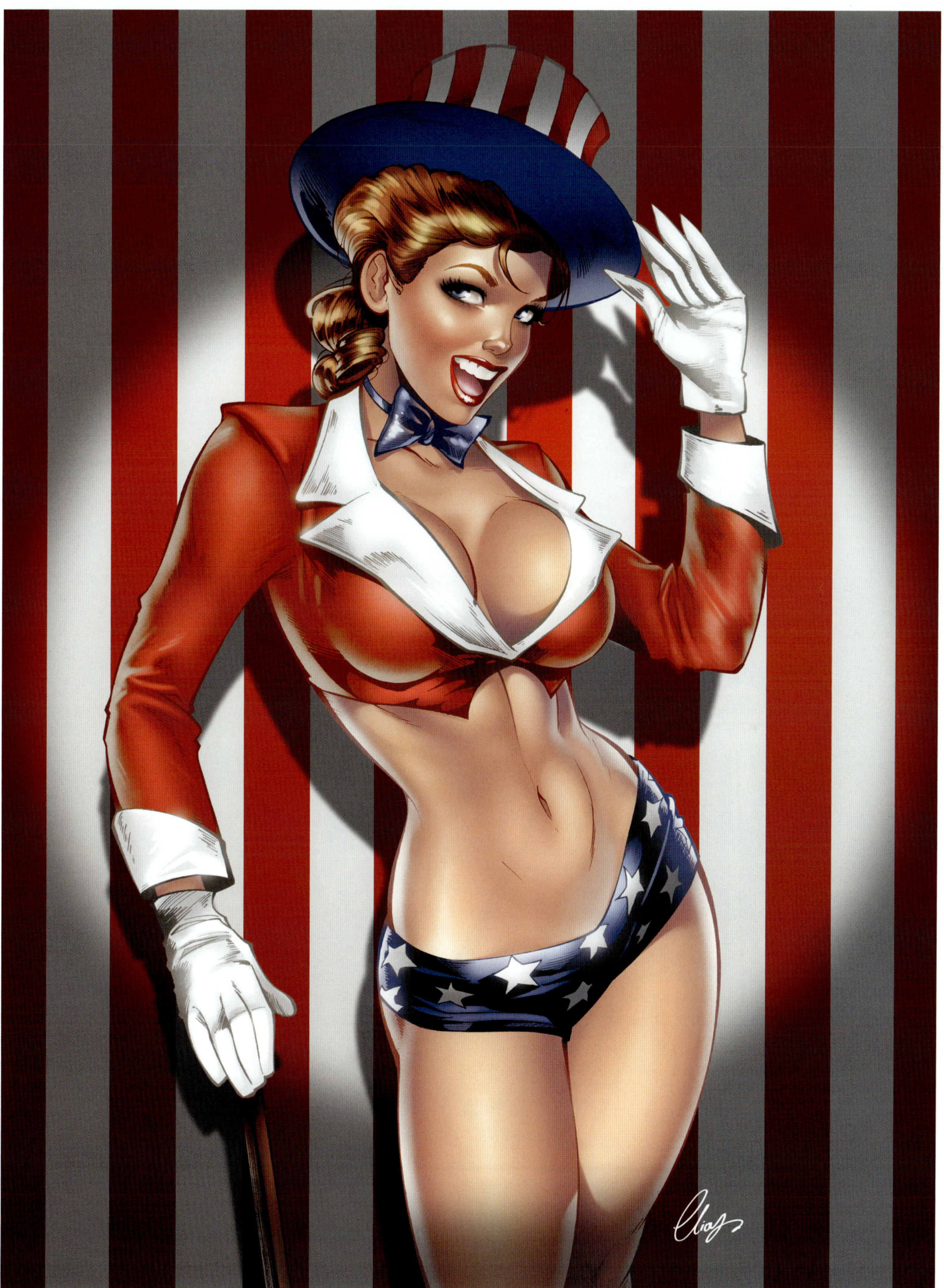

Long Live America!

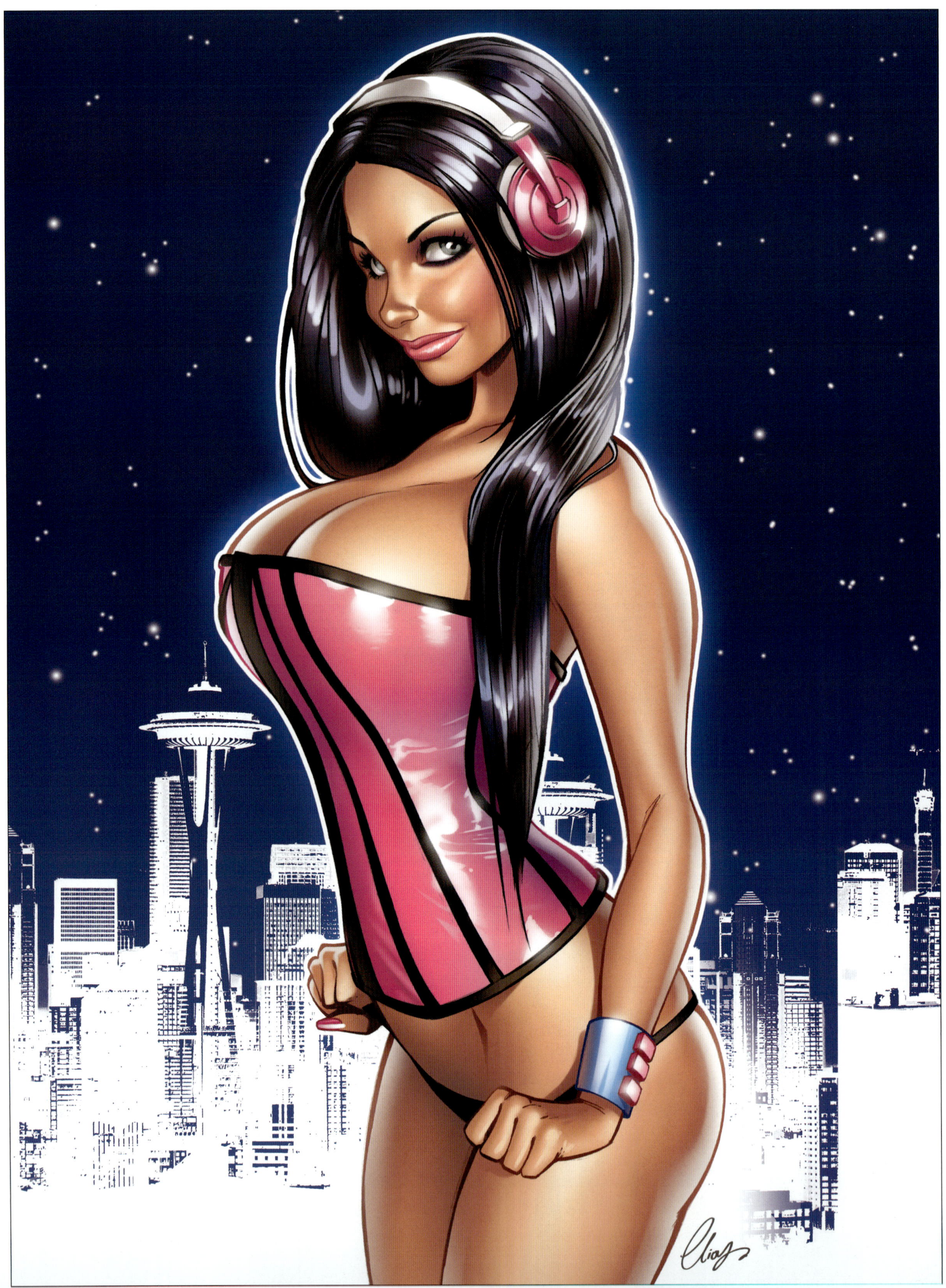

ANGELA

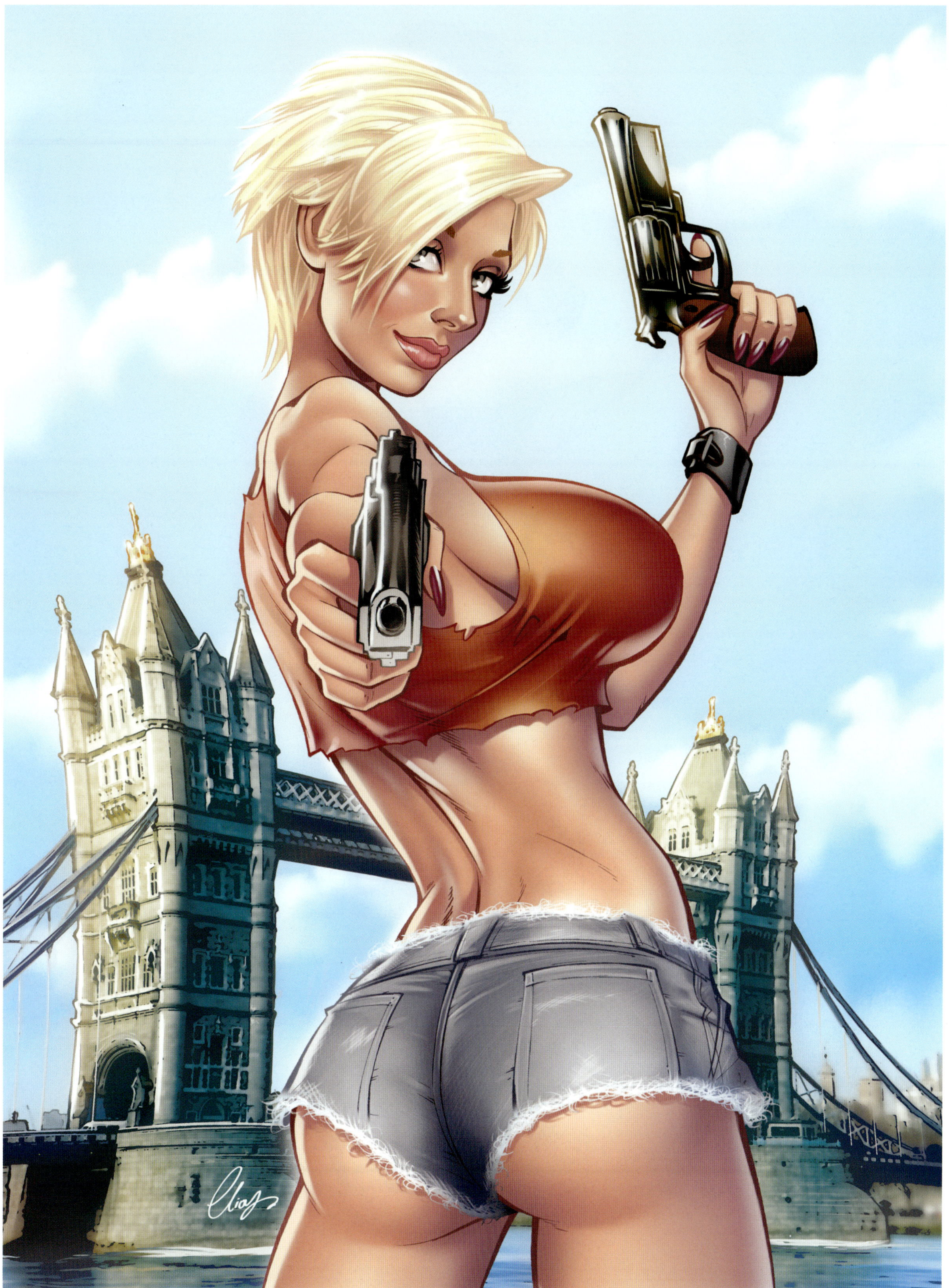

CALUDE

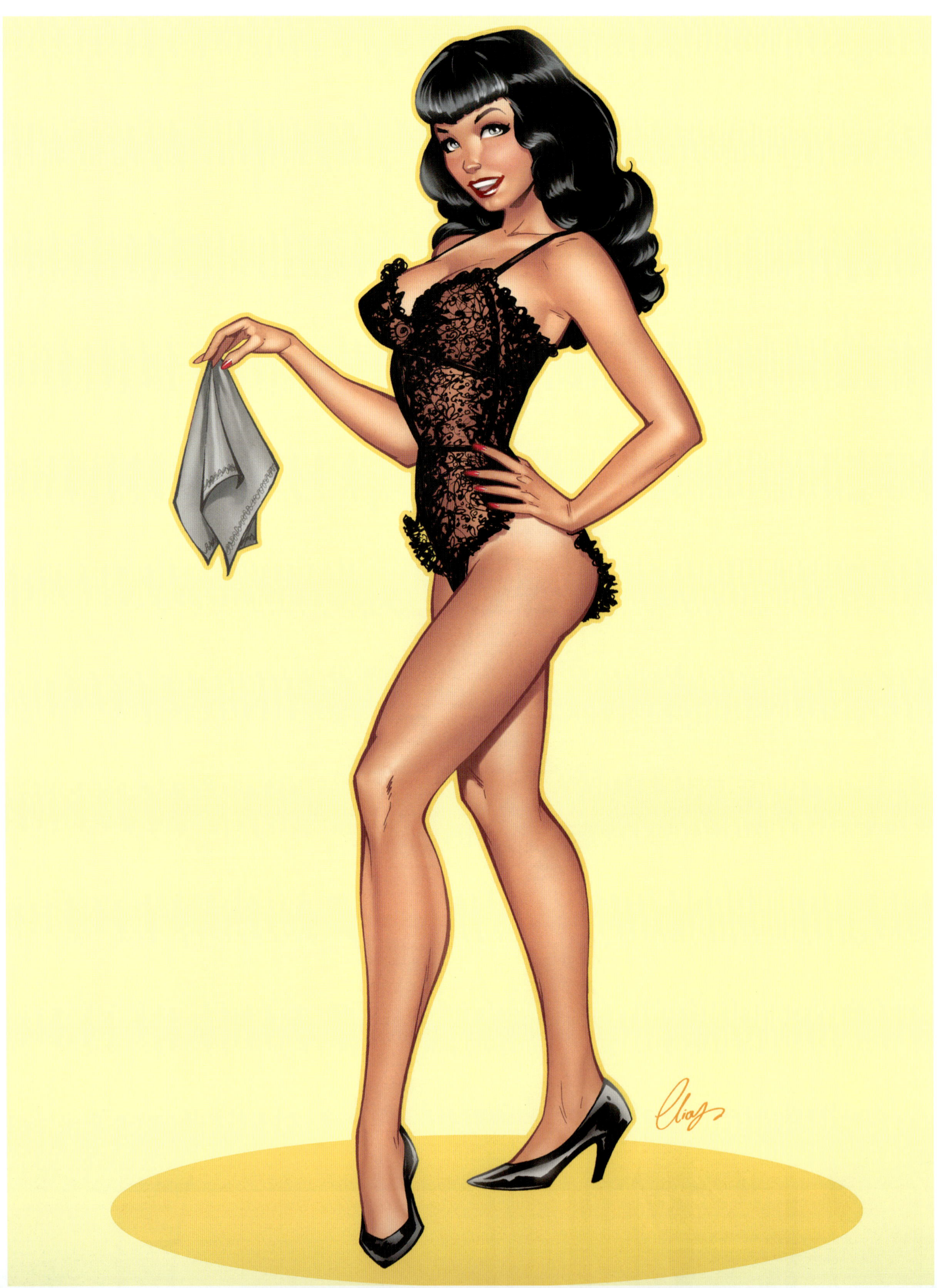

HANKY PANKY

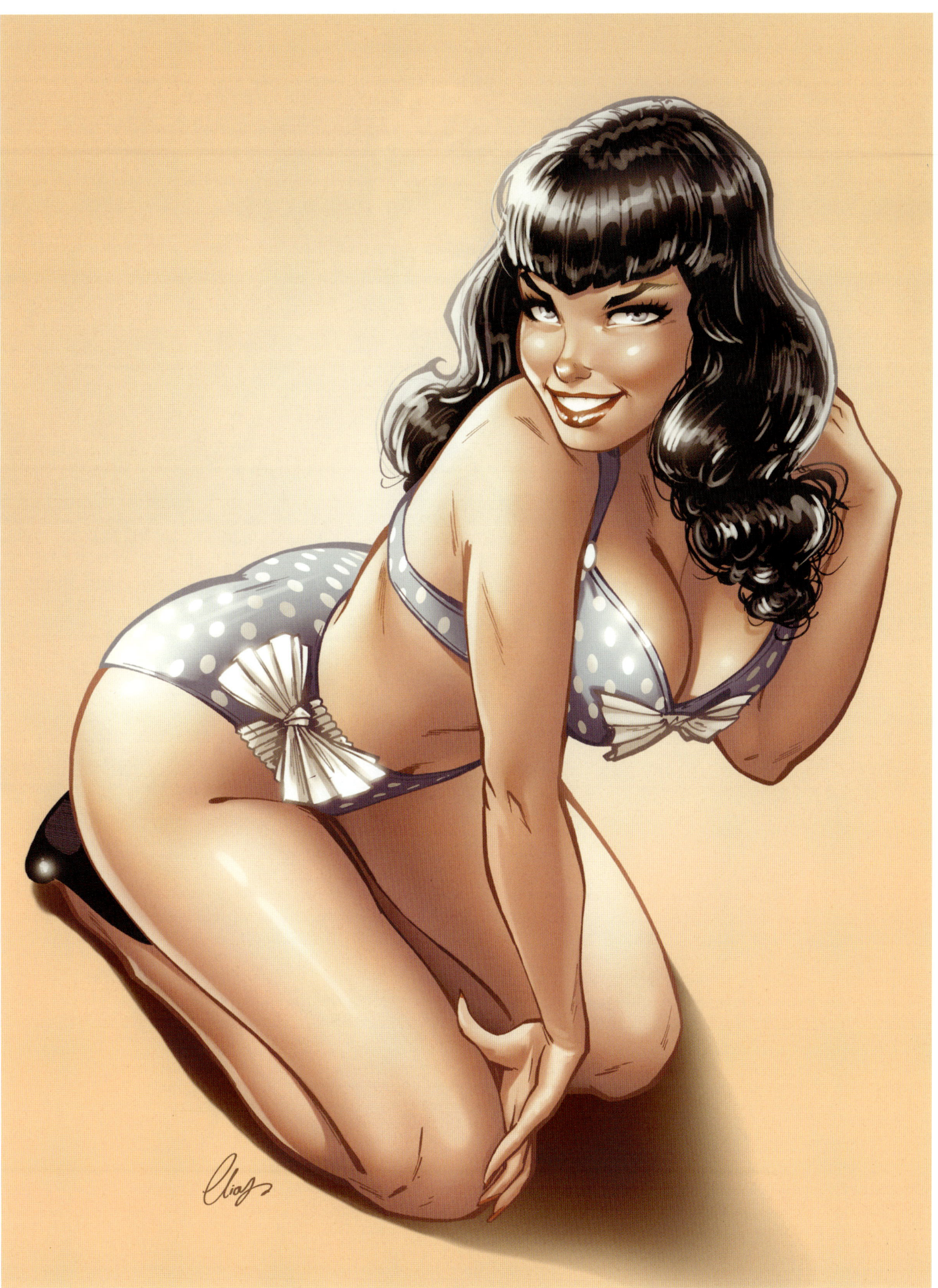

Blast From The Past

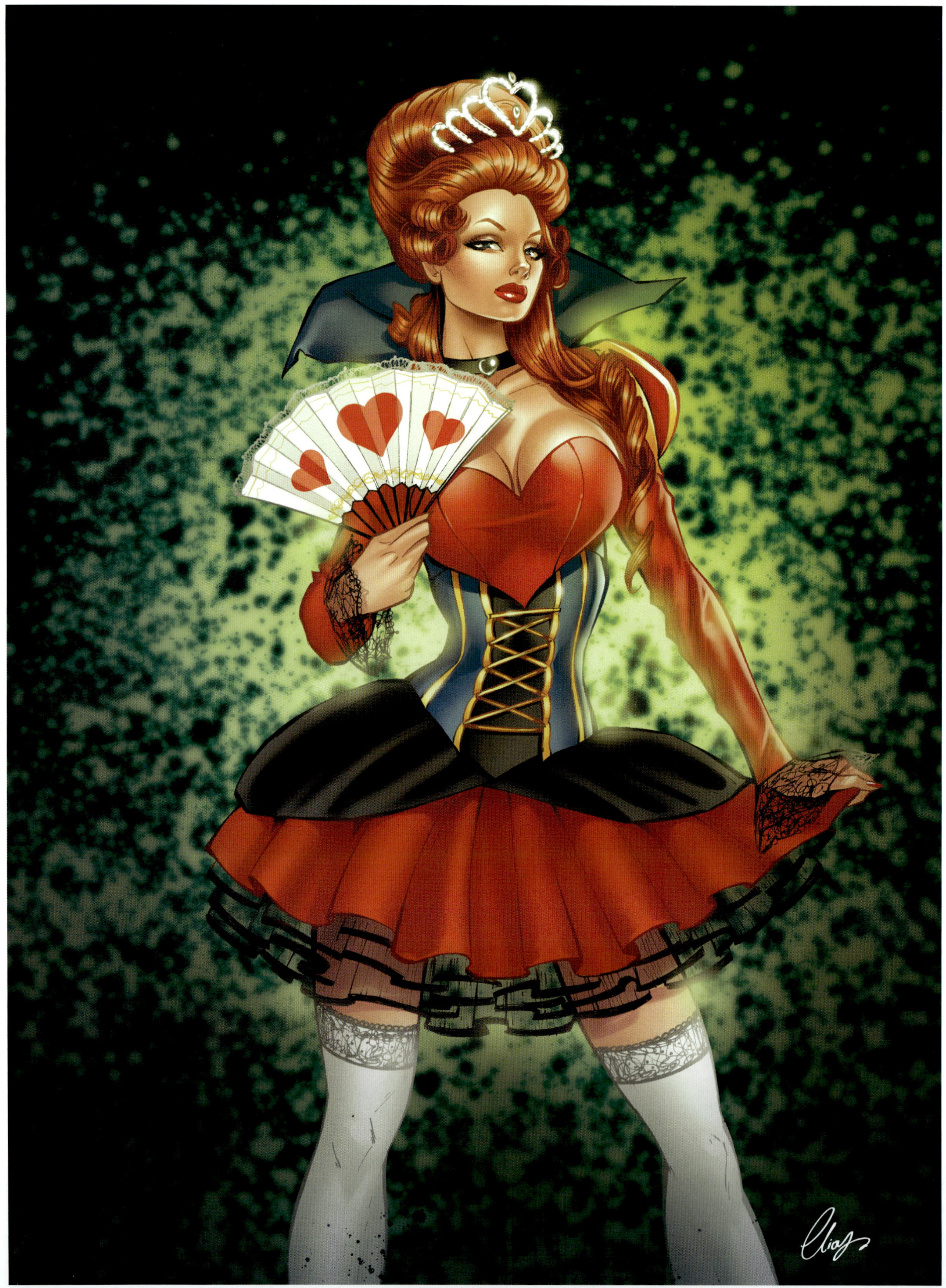

QUEEN OF HEARTS

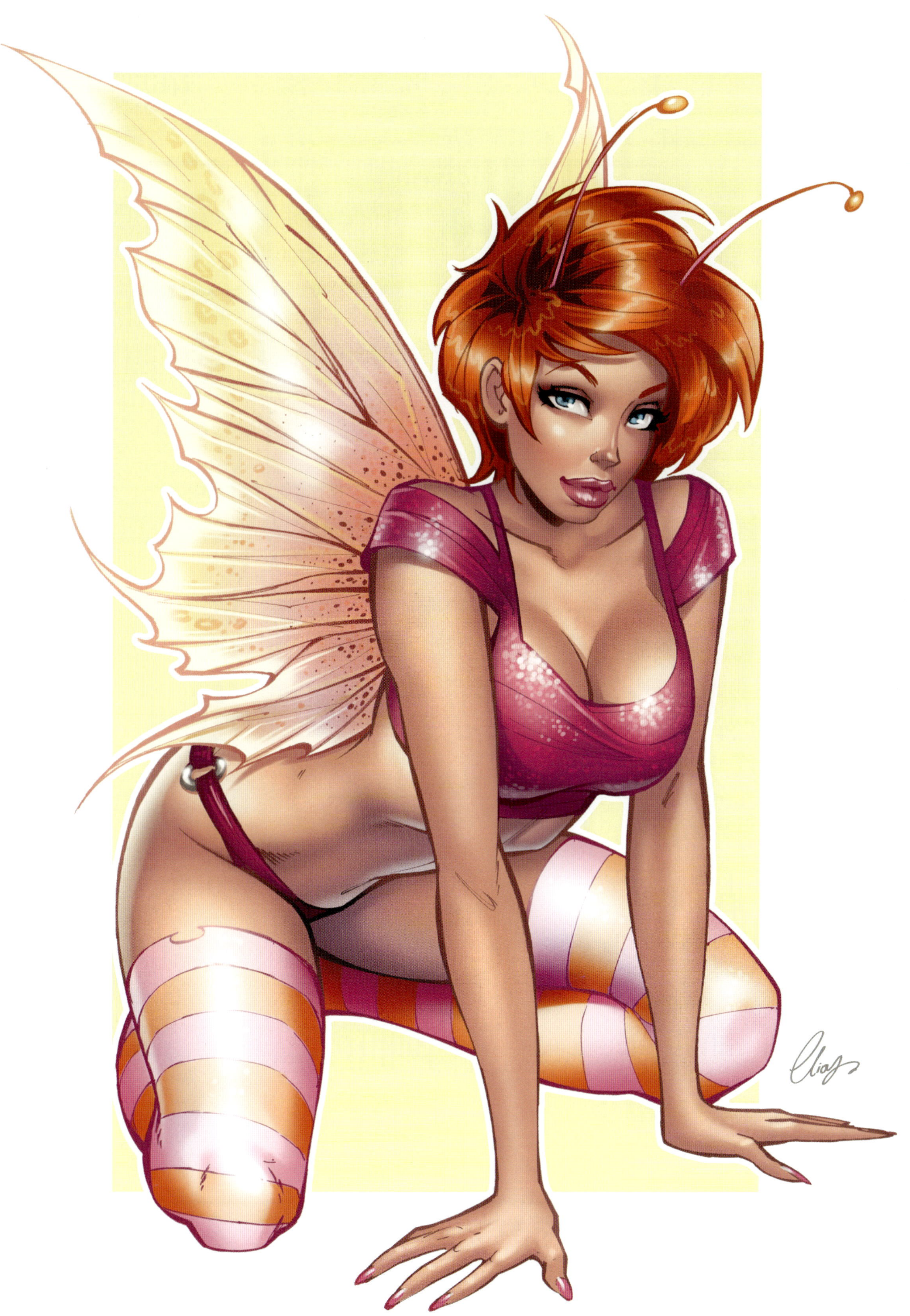

Fairy Jasmine

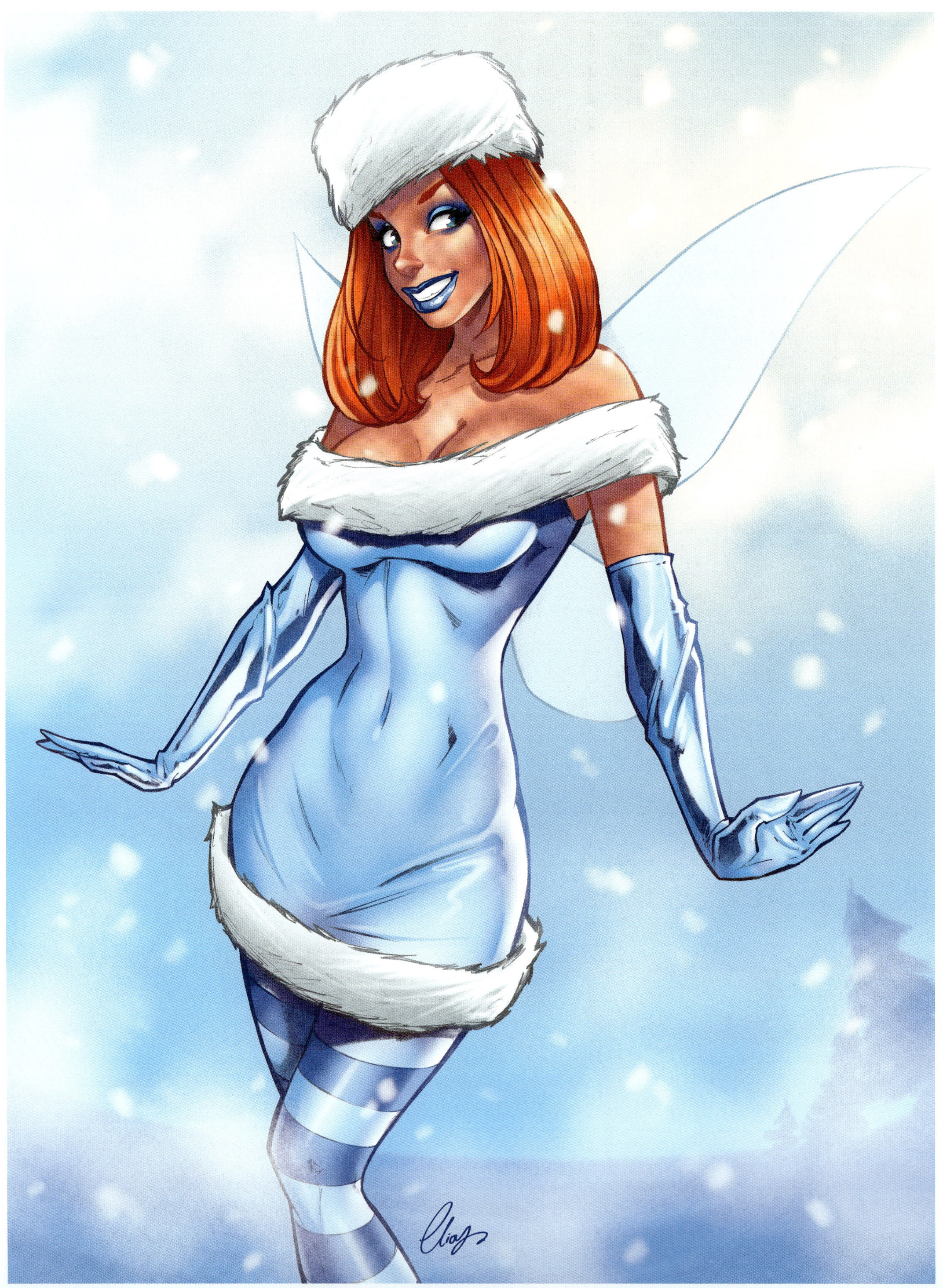

Christmas Fairy

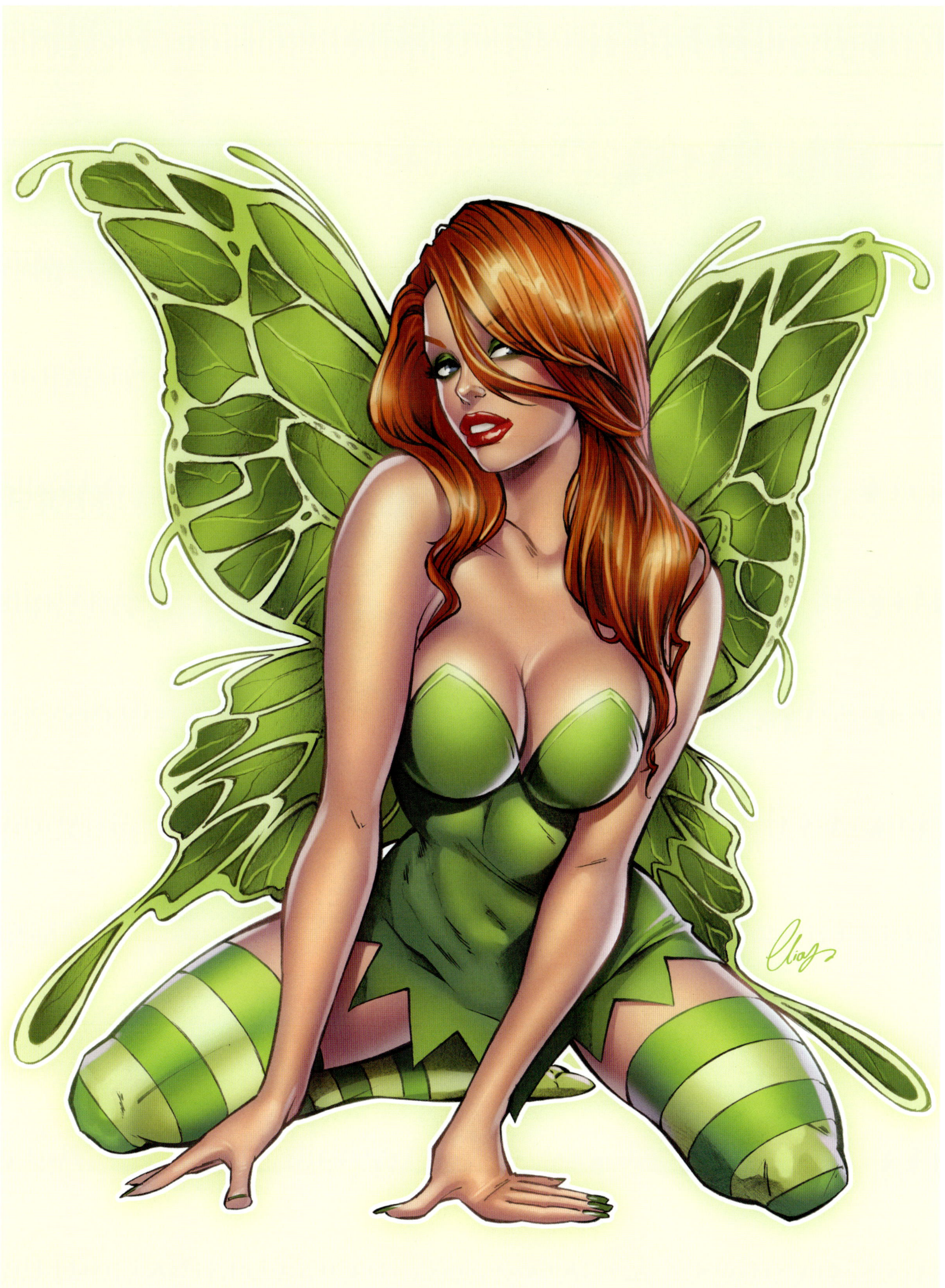

BIMBOBELL

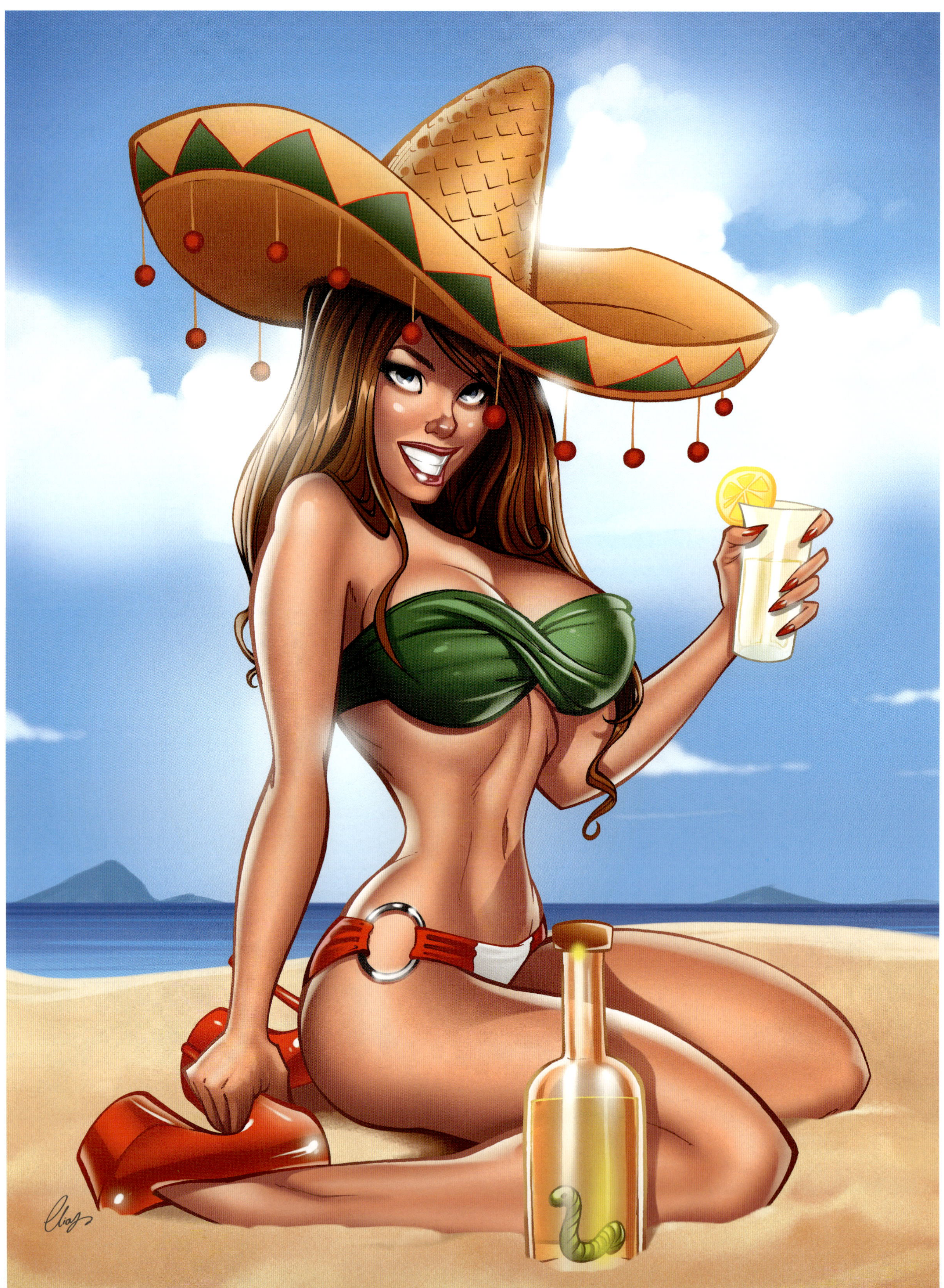

TEQUILA HONEY

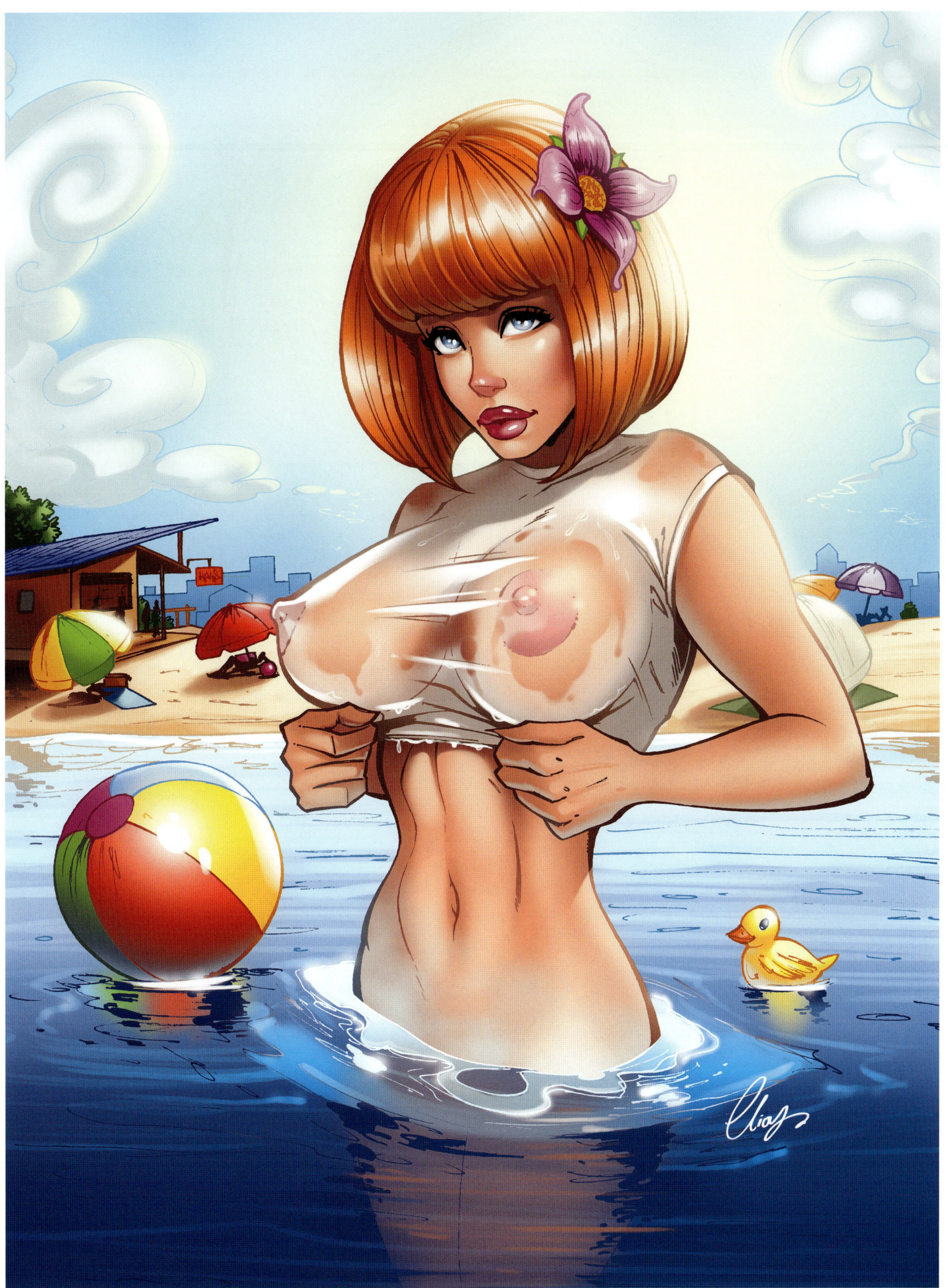

WET SUMMER

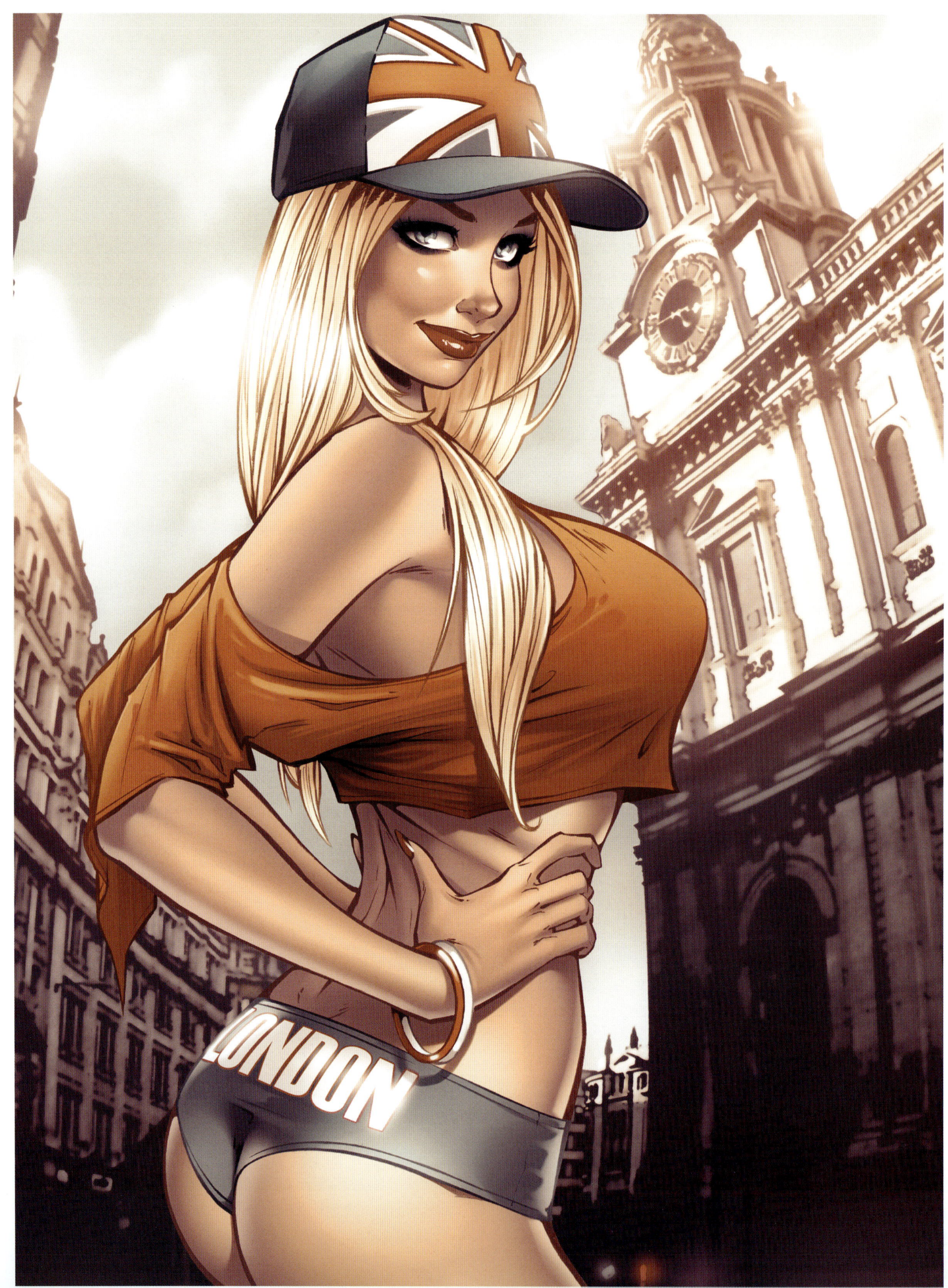

I Love London

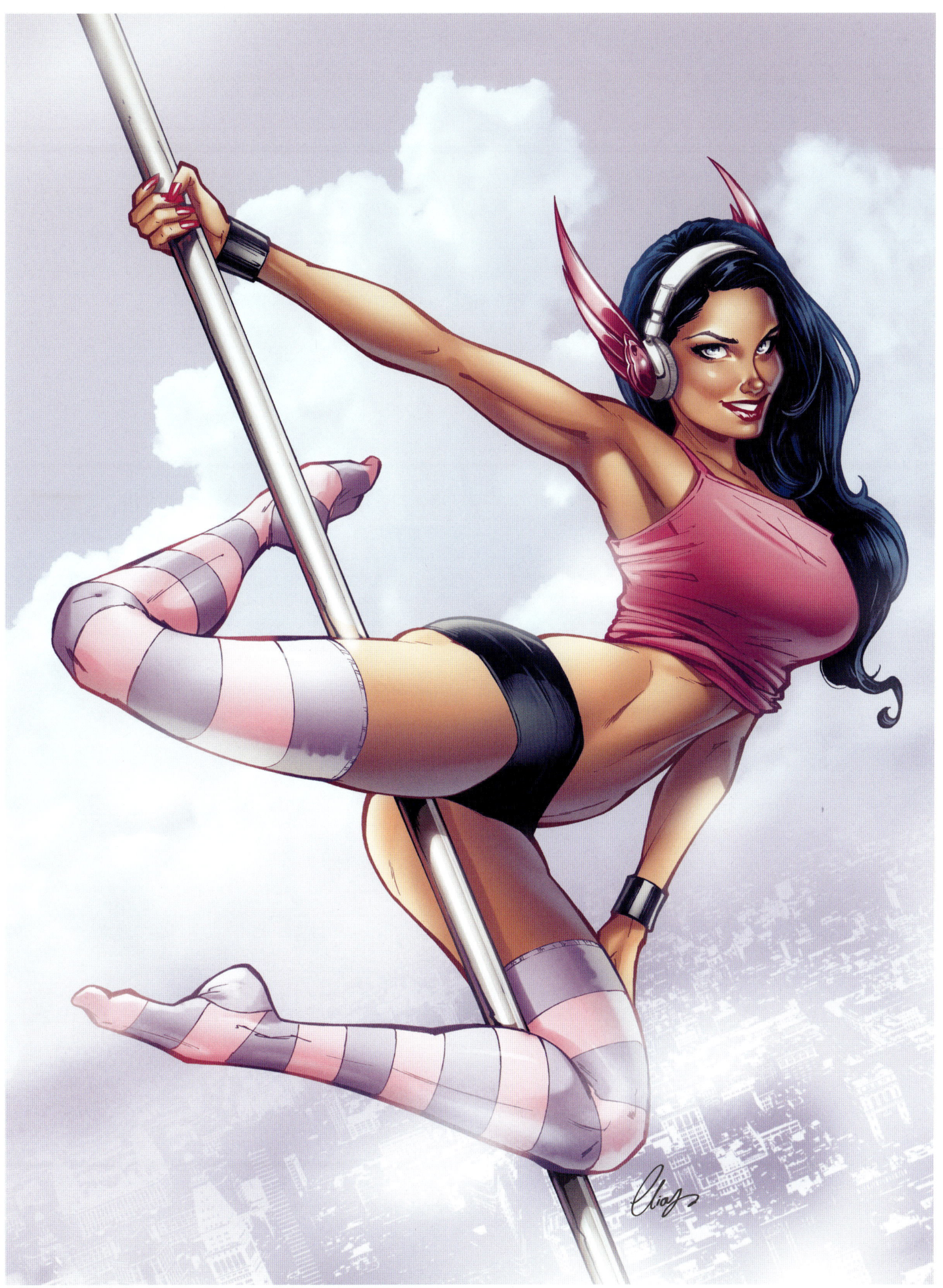

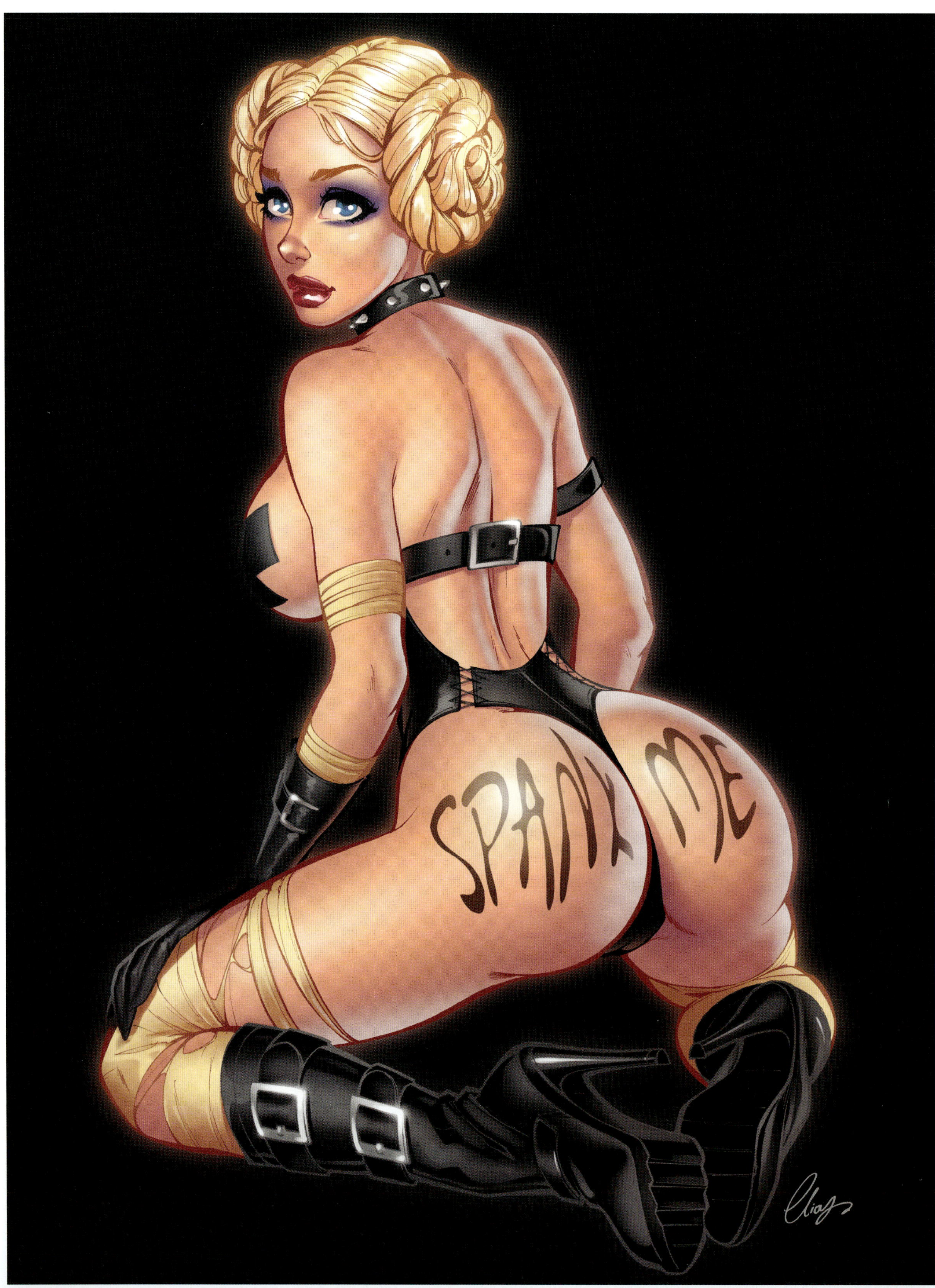

Spank Me